WAKEFIELD AT WORK

PAUL L. DAWSON

AMBERLEY

First published 2020

Amberley Publishing
The Hill, Stroud
Gloucestershire, GL5 4EP

www.amberley-books.com

Cover image is courtesy of Tim Green, CC BY 2.0.

ISBN 978 1 4456 9830 4 (print)
ISBN 978 1 4456 9831 1 (ebook)

British Library Cataloguing in Publication Data.
A catalogue record for this book is available from the British Library.

Origination by Amberley Publishing.
Printed in the UK.

CONTENTS

INTRODUCTION

Wakefield has been a place of habitation for around 6,000 years. The first written evidence for the town comes from the Domesday Book of 1086. The only tangible link we have between the medieval past and the present Wakefield is the layout of its streets and the cathedral, parts of which date back to the twelfth century. Over the past 1,000 years, Wakefield has experienced a period of extensive change, perhaps none more radical than during the early years of the eighteenth century.

Wakefield was for a long time regarded as the capital of the West Riding of Yorkshire (since the Middle Ages), being one of the area's largest population centres until the late eighteenth century. The town had been a parliamentary borough, returning its own MP to London from 1832, and became a municipal borough with a mayor from 1848.

The town was a major centre for cloth dealing and at one time had two piece halls – White Cloth Hall in Westgate and Tammy Hall off King Street. For much of the nineteenth and twentieth centuries, Wakefield had a diverse economy. Textile mills and a large glass works in the east of the city were big employers. There were several collieries around the outskirts of the town and from 1947 the National Coal Board was a major employer. The Eastmoor area was once home to large brickyards. Here, too, was heavy engineering as well as Portland cement production, malting and a thriving trade in soft drinks. E. Green & Sons factory on Calder Vale Road (before moving on to Ossett) was famous for manufacturing the 'Economiser', patented in 1845 by Edward Green. It was a device fitted to a boiler that saves energy by using the exhaust gases from the boiler to preheat the cold water used to fill it. By 2020 all the coal mines and mills (bar one) have closed in recent decades, being replaced by light industrial areas and service centres for international companies.

As well as the cloth trade, Wakefield was a thriving market town. The town was nationally important for its corn and cattle markets, which had been established in 1765. Such was the scale of the business that by 1860 the cattle market was said to be the largest in the north of England, and perhaps Europe. The cattle market closed in the 1960s, but its legacy lives on with the road name Fair Ground Road. Such was the scale of cattle selling that any land suitable for grazing in the immediate environs of the town was turned over to grazing in order to fatten up cows that had been walked over long distances to the market. This raised the price of the land to such a premium it made industrial development uneconomical.

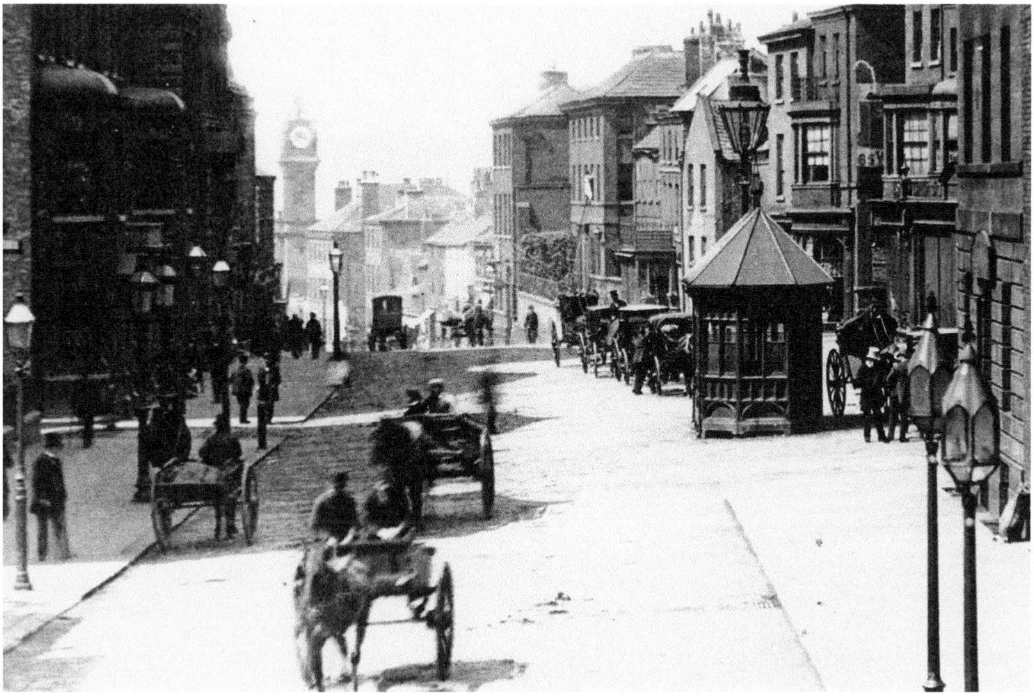

Looking down Westgate in spring 1870. The street is lined with bustling shops. (Yorkshire Archaeological Society)

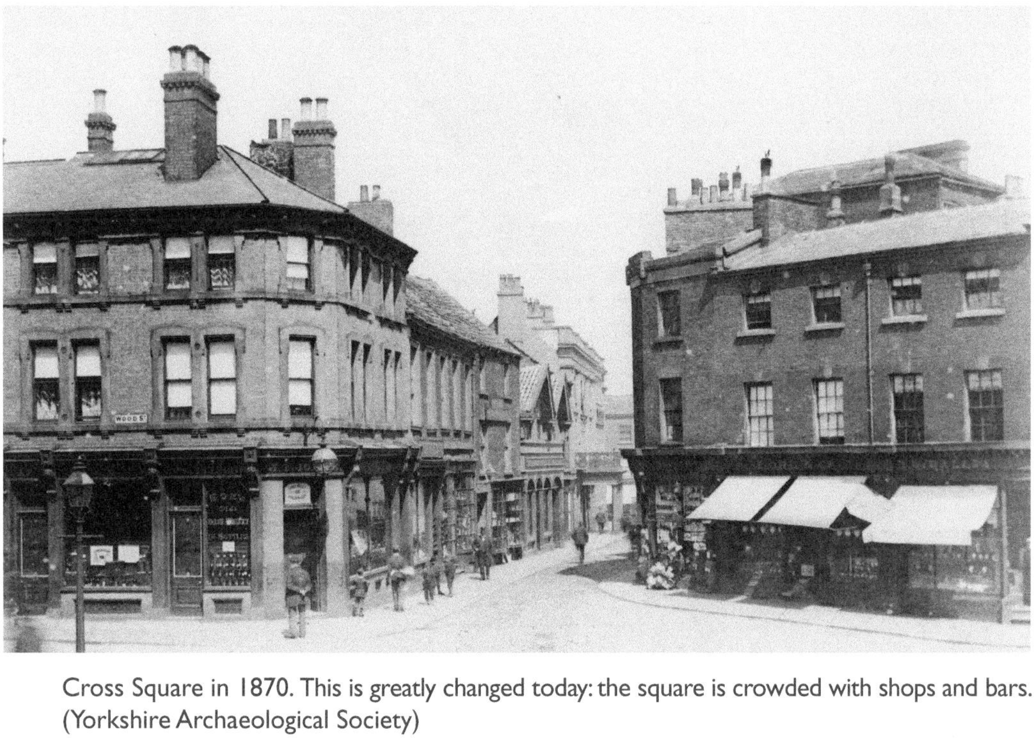

Cross Square in 1870. This is greatly changed today: the square is crowded with shops and bars. (Yorkshire Archaeological Society)

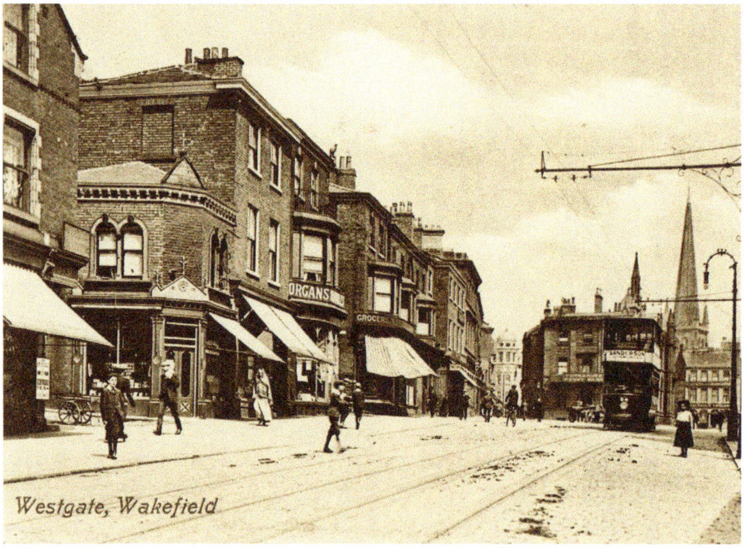

Looking up Westgate in the early twentieth century. Shops and businesses line the street.

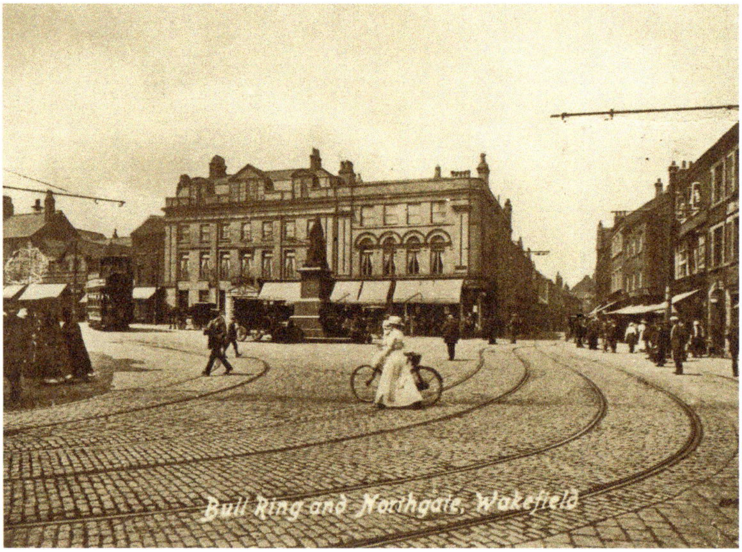

The Bull Ring and Strafford Arms Hotel. The Strafford Arms was an eighteenth-century coaching inn. Wakefield once had a prosperous series of such inns, where stagecoaches changed horses and travellers could eat a brief meal.

Today, Wakefield's commercial base and townscape has fundamentally altered. In the place of mills, factories and open fields are new housing estates to cater for those working elsewhere, like Leeds or Bradford, or empty office park developments. The city also provides jobs in the bar and leisure industry as well as the IT or service industry. Recent development has seen the new shopping centre – Trinity Walk – laid out, a new urban centre at Merchant Gate betwixt Westgate and Balne Lane, as well the impressive £35 million The Hepworth Wakefield art museum, named in honour of local sculptress Barbara Hepworth and opened in May 2011. This book seeks to explore the development of Wakefield's various places of work from the eighteenth century to present times.

Paul L. Dawson BSc (hons), MA, MIFA, FINS

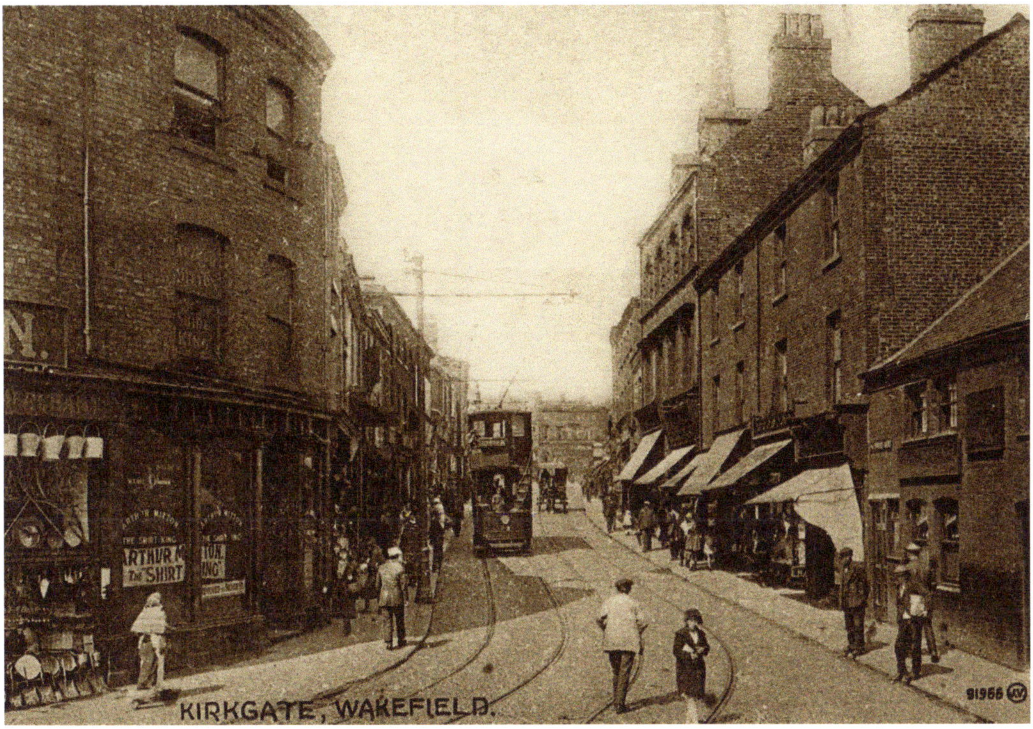

Looking up Kirkgate – crowded with shops and shoppers at the turn of the nineteenth century.

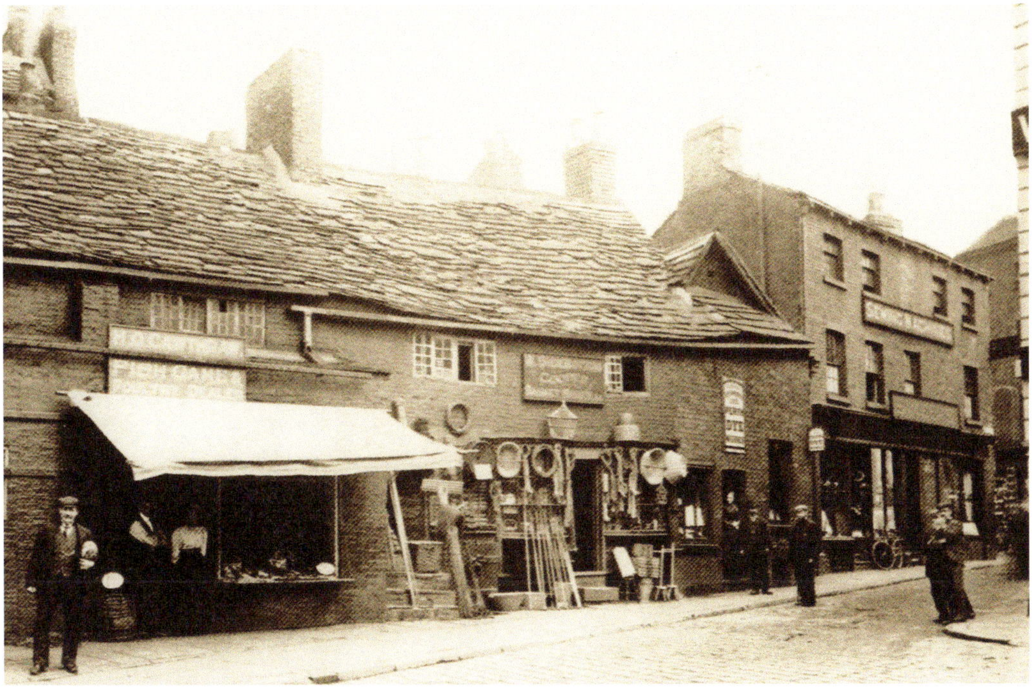

Shops on Marygate *c.* 1880. (Yorkshire Archaeological Society)

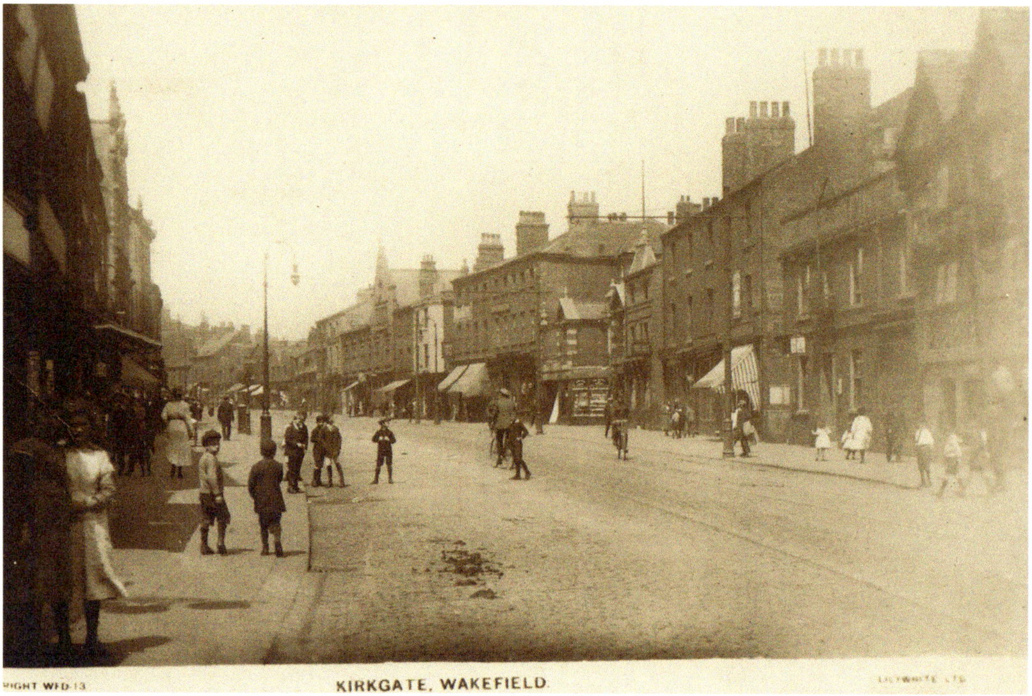

Kirkgate at the turn of the nineteenth century. It was once a busy thoroughfare and retail area in Victorian Wakefield.

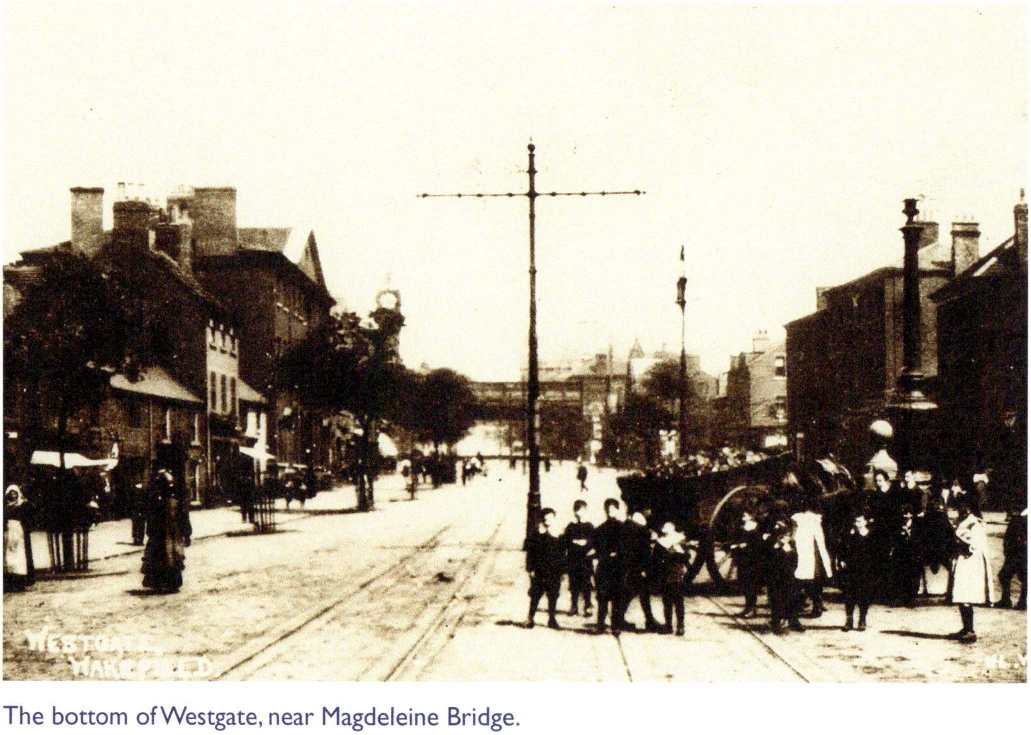

The bottom of Westgate, near Magdeleine Bridge.

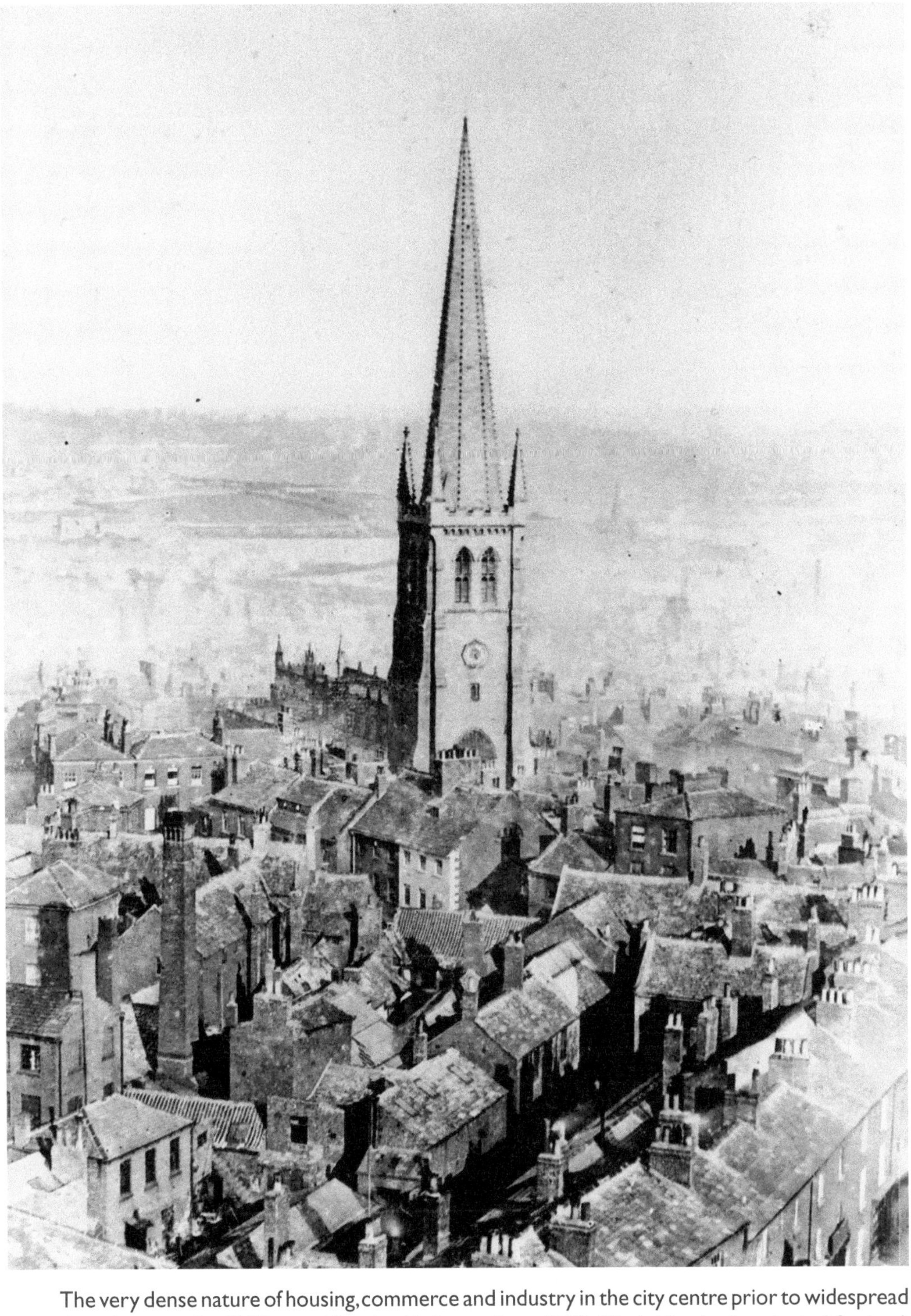

The very dense nature of housing, commerce and industry in the city centre prior to widespread demolition in the 1960s is evident in this image from 1870. (Yorkshire Archaeological Society)

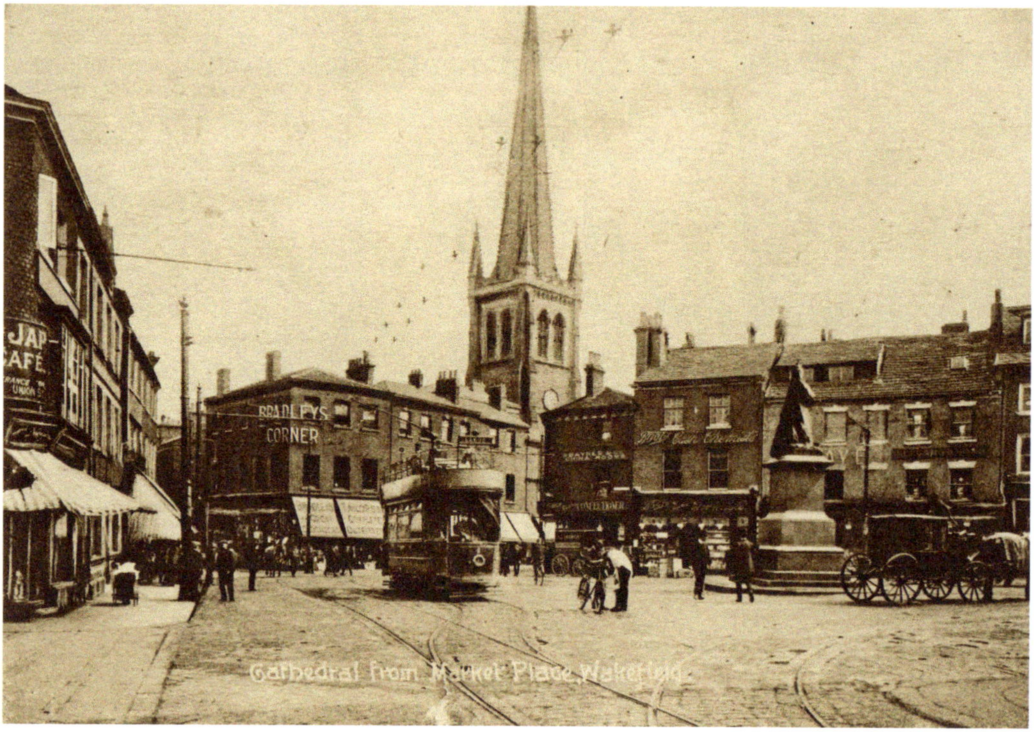

The Bull Ring around 1910 – crowded with shoppers looking for a bargain.

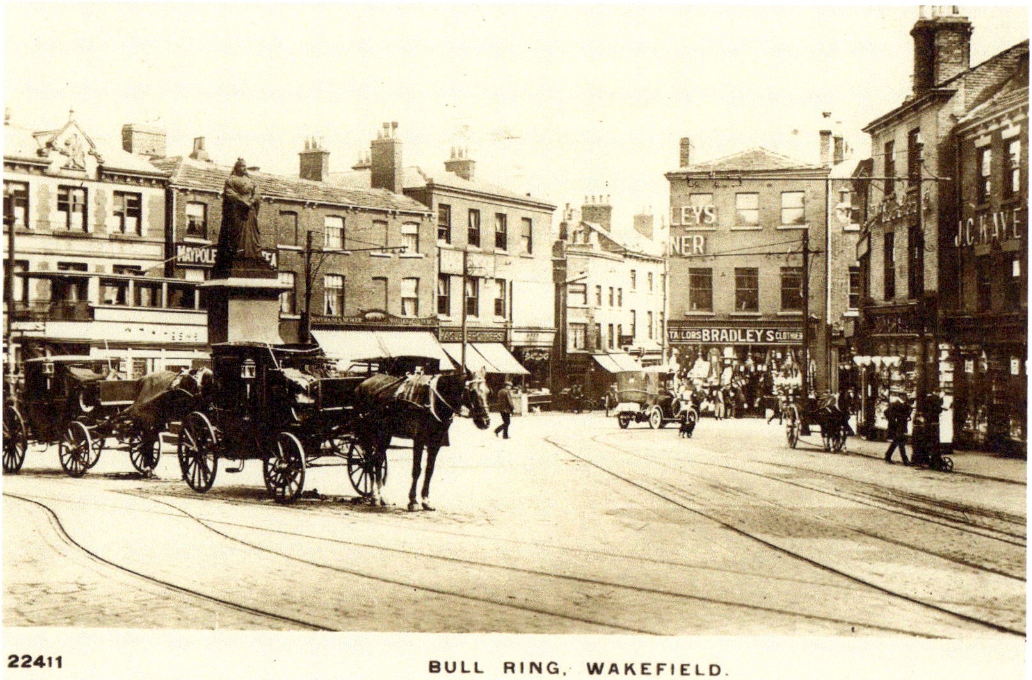

The Bull Ring, the commercial hub of the city in the years before the First World War.

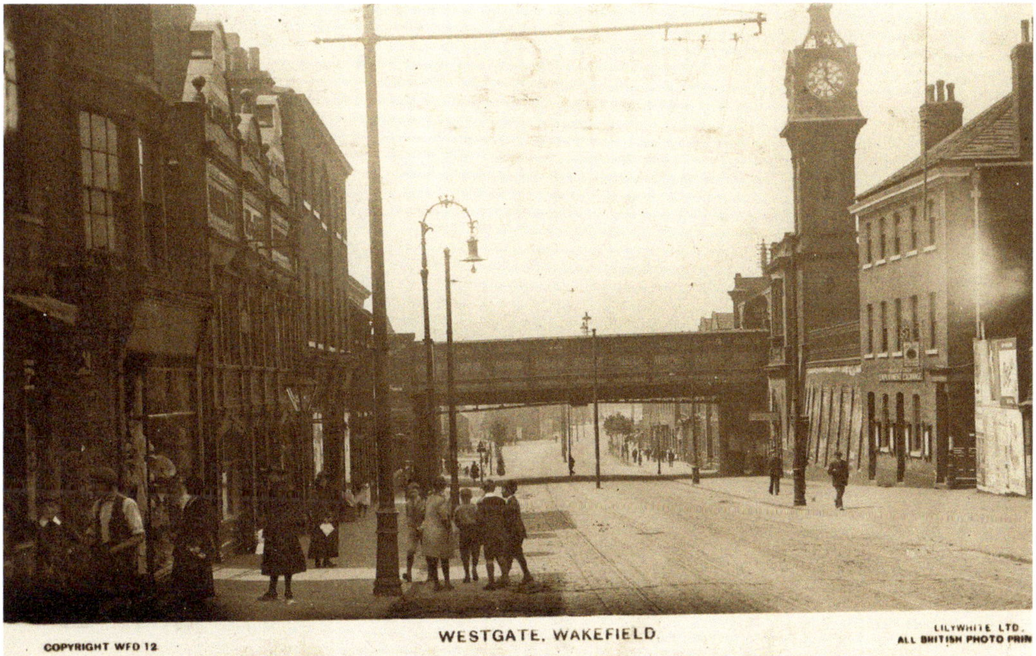

The Elephant and Castle public house and Hoffmans the butchers can be seen on the left of the image. The long-demolished clock tower of Westgate station is to the right.

EIGHTEENTH-CENTURY CLOTH PRODUCTION

Historians favour the term 'proto-industrialisation' to describe the form of industrial organisation that emerged in the sixteenth century. The word was initially applied to cottage industries in the countryside. In spite of the opposition of urban guilds, rural residents were performing many industrial tasks. Agricultural labour did not occupy the peasantry for the entire year, and spare time, if such a concept existed, was put to such activities as spinning wool or weaving and washing cloth. Peasants usually worked for lower remuneration than urban artisans. Protoindustrialisation gave rural residents supplementary income, which conferred a certain immunity from harvest failures; it enabled them to marry younger and rear larger families; and it prepared them, socially and psychologically, for eventual industrialisation. The efforts of urban guilds to limit rural work enjoyed only limited success. In England, for example, the restrictions seem rarely to have been enforced. Cottage industries certainly existed in the Middle Ages, but the economic expansion of the sixteenth and seventeenth centuries diffused them over much larger areas of the European countryside, perhaps most visibly in England and western Germany.

More recently, historians have stressed the role of towns in this early form of industrial organisation. Towns remained the centres from which the raw materials were distributed into the countryside. In Wakefield, for example, the raw wool market sold fleece to those who would card and spin the fleece into yarn. The yarn was then sold to the weavers. The urban centre was also the distribution point for the finished cloth for sale to merchants. Weaving and spinning in the seventeenth and eighteenth centuries, into the nineteenth century in the West Riding, was a rural-based cottage industry until the advent of the factory system. Moreover, urban entrepreneurs like the Milnes family coordinated the efforts of the rural workers and marketed their finished products. Certain processes – usually the most highly skilled and the most remunerative – remained centred in urban centres. Cloth finishing and dyeing was a skilled activity and was centred in Wakefield for a large proportion of the West Riding in the Calder and Aire valleys. The extension of industry into rural areas and the greater integration of urban and rural industry into regional economies was the principal achievement of sixteenth-century industry.

This manner of organising manufactures is known as the 'putting-out system', an awkward translation of the German Verlagssystem. The key to its operation was the entrepreneur, who purchased the raw materials, distributed them among the working families, passed the semi-finished products from one artisan to another, and marketed the finished products. He was typically a great merchant resident in the town like Richard Milnes (1696–1755).

The economic base of Wakefield was the cloth trade, and had been from the time of Henry VIII – if not earlier. The trade became dominated during the eighteenth century by the merchant prince families – the Heywoods, Milnes and Naylors. The Milnes family were successful cloth and wine merchants and various branches of the family owned houses on Westgate. In the later eighteenth century the Holdsworth family built their fortune in the dyeing of cloth. The principal activity of the town at this period was the dressing and finishing of woollen cloth. Undyed and unfinished cloths were sent to Wakefield to be dyed and finished before being dispatched to London or the Continent. The nominal head of the family was Pemberton Milnes. Pemberton Milnes (1729–95) was born on 27 September 1729, son of Richard Milnes (1696–1755) and Bridget Pemberton. He married Jane Slater in January 1754 – his brother Robert's wife's sister. Known in his own lifetime as Pem Milnes, he was brought up in the family's cloth merchanting business. His elder brother Robert (1708–71) was the father of Richard Slater Milnes, known as Dick by his stepmother. Richard Milnes' younger brother John was the father of Jack Milnes the Democrat; Sir Robert Shore Milnes, deputy governor general of Lower Canada, and Hannah Milnes, courtesan. Jack, Richard and Pemberton dominated the commerce of Wakefield for over fifty years.

Pemberton Milnes had his name inserted into the Commission for the Peace on 25 May 1762, with John Milnes and Robert Milnes inserted as JPs the same day, although they never seem to have acted. He took his dedimus (a writ to commission private persons to do some act in place of a judge, such as to examine a witness, etc.) on 7 June 1765, the same day as John Milnes, but neither went on to swear oaths. Pemberton swore his oath at Rotherham in July 1770. His decision to act was probably influenced by the Marquis of Rockingham in light of the coining affair of 1769–70 to see more JPs in the manufacturing area of the West Riding. He was appointed the same day as Revd Henry Zouch, Richard Wilson and Joshua Horton – all four men had taken their oaths over five years since being inserted into the Commission of the Peace was unprecedented. Pemberton was the second most active JP in the West Riding after Henry Zouch. His father Richard Milnes had been inserted into the Commission of the Peace 22 October 1736, and his dedimus on 27 January 1744. Pemberton Milnes was also a deputy lieutenant of Yorkshire. He was also a major player in politics. He was a frequent correspondent with the Marquis of Rockingham and his successor, Earl Fitzwilliam. He owned land in several counties and used his influence to mobilise the vote for the Whig cause. He supported the American Colonists in 1776, in direct contrast to his erstwhile cousin Banastre Tarleton.

Pemberton Milnes was one of the first committee men of the Wakefield Library (established in 1786) and subscribed to the York Emanuel Charity Fund (formed in 1782). He became guardian for his nephew Richard Slater Rich upon his father's death. He was recognised as the leader of Yorkshire dissent, and managed to combine the duties of magistrate, merchant, banker and landowner, as well reportedly being the largest consumer of port in the county. He built Bawtry Hall as his main residence in 1779. He continued his interest in the cloth trade, and was a committee member for the building of a new White Cloth Hall in Leeds in 1774, as well as being chairman of the Joint-Stock Ossett Mill Company in the 1780s. The roof trusses for Westgate Chapel were brought back from the Baltic – the Milnes family had the sole contract to clothe the Russian army, and the timber was a back cargo.

The family financially supported the establishment of the first avowedly Unitarian Chapel in London in the mid-1770s. The leading lights of the congregation were the Dukes of Richmond and Norfolk, Sir George Savile, the Duke of Grafton and Attorney General Lee. His only child, Mary Bridgette Milnes (1754–1835), married firstly P. A. Hay Drummond,

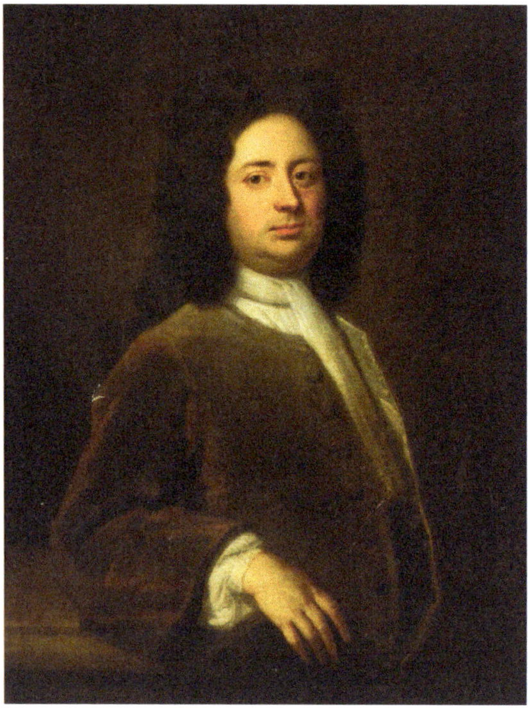

Richard Milnes (1696–1755), political ally of the 1st Marquis of Rockingham, was the scion of the Milnes dynasty of Wakefield. He lies beneath Westgate Chapel in the catacombs.

son of the Archbishop of York and then Viscount Galway in 1803. His widow, Jane, died on 21 September 1812, aged eighty-one. Pemberton himself died in 1795 at his sister's house. Pemberton's house was threatened with being firebombed by the 'church and king mob' for his left-wing political views at the height of anti-French and anti-Revolutionary fervour in England at the time. The Milnes family were all out and out Jacobins or sympathisers to the ideals of the French Revolution. Pemberton fled the house and died of shock. His firm, Milnes, Heywood & Company, established in the 1770s continued and dominated for a time the Yorkshire cloth trade.

As trade routes grew longer, the small artisan was placed at ever-greater distances from sources of supply and from markets. Typically, the small artisan would not have the knowledge of distant markets or of the preferences of distant purchasers and rarely had the money to purchase needed raw materials. The size of the trading networks and the volume of merchandise moving within them made the services of the entrepreneur indispensable and subordinated the workers to his authority. In Wakefield, the Milnes family imported raw fleece from Germany and from Lancashire. The family then 'put out' the raw materials to rural producers. The domestic system differed from the handicraft system of home production in that the workers neither bought materials nor sold products. It undermined the restrictive regulations of the urban guilds and brought the first widespread industrial employment of women and children. The process in the making of wool for clothes was as follows: cleaning of the wool after it had been sheared from the sheep. carding of the wool – this was brushing it to separate the fibres. Carding was usually done by children. This involved using a hand-card that removed and untangled the short fibres from the mass. Hand cards were essentially wooden blocks fitted with handles and covered with short metal spikes. The spikes were angled and set in leather. The fibres were worked between the spikes and, be reversing the cards, scrapped off in rolls (cardings) about 12 inches long and just under an inch thick. If a comb was used, this would be to get the fibres parallel. The cleaned and carded wool would then be spun by spinsters. This was frequently done by young girls. If these girls had not got married at a young age, it was believed that they would remain unmarried all their life – hence the term spinster today. The finished product of the spinsters was called yarn. It was the carding cleaning and spinning of the fleece into yarn which was the first part of cloth production to be mechanised. In Wakefield that began with Ebenezer Aldred in 1781. Daniel Defoe commented in 1724 that:

> 'The nearer we came to Halifax, we found the houses thicker, and the villages greater. The sides of hills, which were very steep, were spread with houses; for the land being divided into small enclosures, that is to say, from two acres to six or seven acres each, seldom more; every three or four pieces of land had a house belonging to it.
> Their business is the clothing trade. Each clothier must keep a horse, perhaps two, to fetch and carry for the use of his manufacture, to fetch home his wool and his provisions from the market, to carry his yarn to the spinners, his manufacture to the fulling mill, and, when finished, to the market to be sold.
> Among the manufacturers' houses are likewise scattered an infinite number of cottages or small dwellings, in which dwell the workmen which are employed, the women and children of whom, are always busy carding, spinning, etc. so that no hands being unemployed all can gain their bread, even from the youngest to the ancient; anyone above four years old works.

Once it has been spun, the thread was then passed on to weavers to make into cloth – one such family were the Shuttleworths of Outwood. The finished products were returned to the employers for payment on a piecework or wage basis.

Each of these processes probably took place in separate cottages and spinning was seen as a job for women, while weaving was seen as a man's job. If an artisan did not work in his own home, he might work in a small workshop. Everything was done on a small scale. Even the coal mines – to fuel local cottages rather than send coal further afield – were small with shallow bell pits being the favoured type of mine as opposed to deep coal mining. The cloth was then finished at the fulling mill, cropping shops and dye works before it was sold to the internal market or for export. The Milnes family also bought cloth that had been produced by other weavers in the domestic system. The Milnes bought hundreds if not thousands of lengths of loom finished cloth, and processed it into saleable product. As the eighteenth century progressed, the Milnes family shifted from that of cloth finisher to entrepreneur. This resulted in the establishment of factories. In the seventeenth and eighteenth centuries, such was the division of labour that many entrepreneurs concentrated solely on the processing of fleece into yarn and the production of cloth, which were sold in the West Riding at the vast piece halls of Huddersfield, Halifax and Leeds. George Walker commented in 1814:

> The manufacture of cloth affords employment to the major part of the lower class of people in the north-west districts of the West Riding of Yorkshire. These cloth-makers reside almost entirely in the villages, and bring their cloth on market-days for sale in the great halls erected for that purpose at Leeds and Huddersfield.

The woven cloth was sold to merchants called clothiers who visited the village with their trains of packhorses. These men became the first capitalists. The finishing of the cloth was left

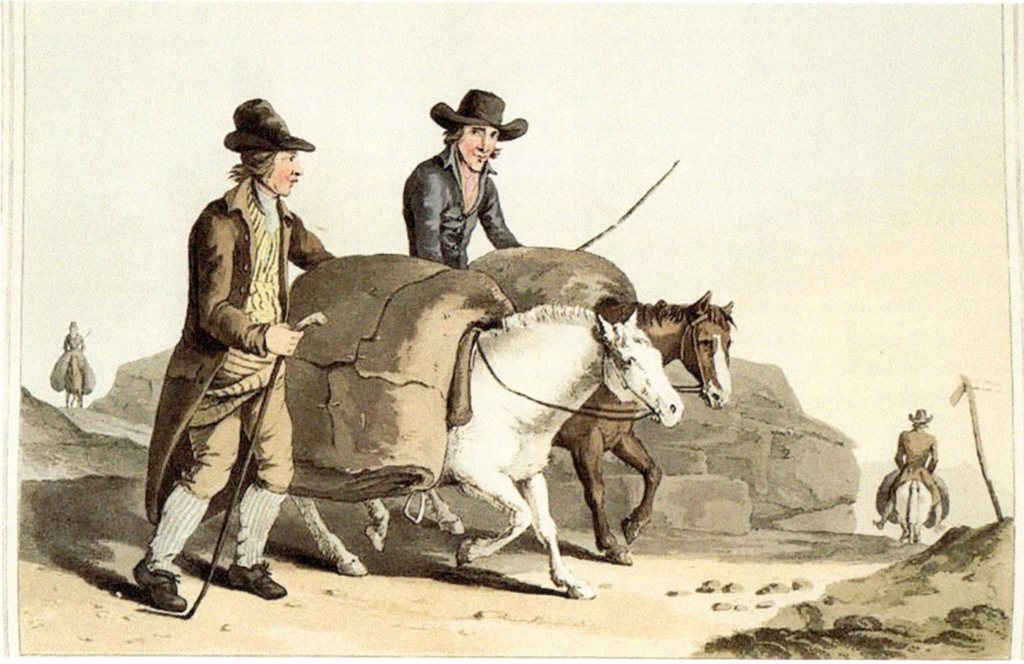

A print dated 1814 of a clothier taking his finished cloth to market. This scene was an everyday occurrence in Wakefield for over 200 years.

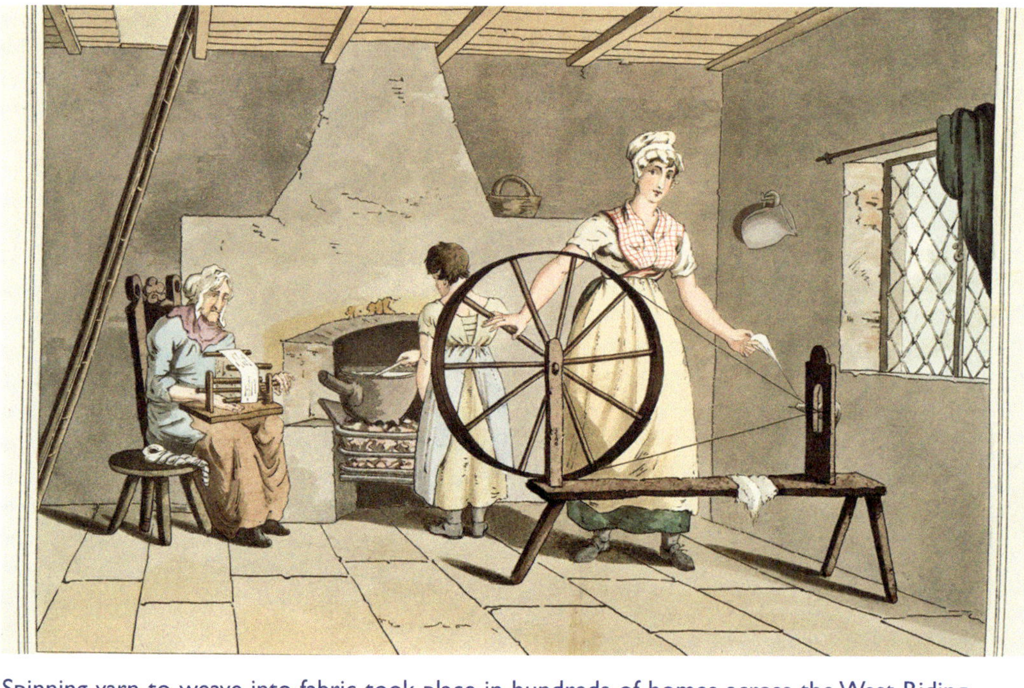

Spinning yarn to weave into fabric took place in hundreds of homes across the West Riding as part of the domestic system of cloth production. It came to an end by the 1850s through large-scale industrialisation.

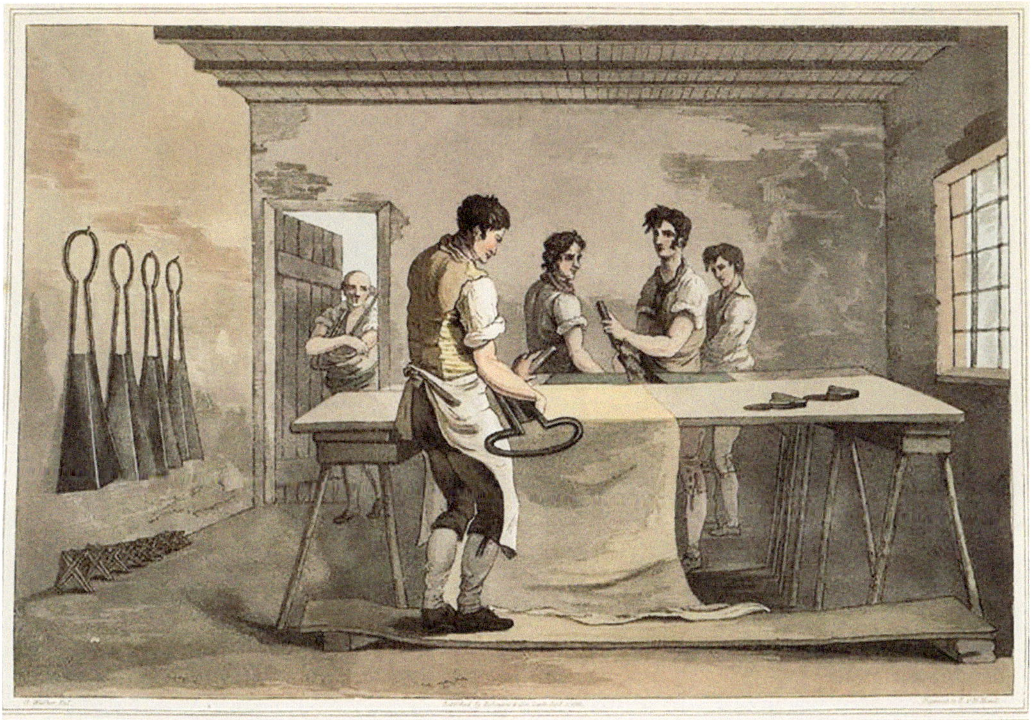

Before mechanisation, cloth finishing was a very skilled trade. In Wakefield, huge profits were made by the Milnes and Naylor families in processing raw cloth into a finished product. The Scott family of Scott's Yard, Westgate (roughly where Emerald way is today) was the site of their business premises. They were the premier cloth dressers of the town.

to others – the great cloth merchants. They employed specialist croppers, finishers and dyers. Wakefield was a centre for such work.

To reduce costs and to speed up production time, by 1780 the cloth merchants were now concentrating all the differing trades under their direct supervision. We start to see merchants themselves becoming involved in the manufacture of yarn and cloth- the merchants with an average income of £10,0000 compared to an annual income for £18 for a soldier, had the fiscal capacity to invest in machinery and buildings. Yet despite this, the domestic system held its own until the 1850's when steam powered looms took gained the upper hand. The Milnes family were the drivers of change in the West Riding along with the Ackroyd and Atkinsons families of Halifax and Huddersfield respectively. Before the Industrial Revolution any growth in productivity or output was limited by the small-scale nature of many manufacturing activities. In the woollen textile industry, for example, processes were highly specialised and scattered across the country, centred on domestic manufacturing carried out in the homes of workers. Early technical innovations continued to depend on this 'putting-out' system as a form of commercial organisation. Initial technical developments in spinning and weaving (such as John Kay's 'flying shuttle') thus remained relatively small-scale, with new machinery still operated by just one pair of hands.

The mercantile development of Wakefield in the eighteenth century was dominated by Westgate Chapel and the families that worshiped within its walls. Westgate Chapel was the first place of worship built in Wakefield since the Reformation. The first chapel was opened in 1697 on Westgate Common. The current building dates from 1752. The theology of the congregation evolved over the course of the eighteenth century from trinitarian Christianity to Unitarianism – the denial of Jesus as part of the Godhead. The cloth trade had been the lifeblood of Wakefield since the sixteenth century. Within the walls of Westgate Chapel gathered the leading cloth merchants – the Milnes, Lumbs, Naylors and, for a time, the Charnocks. It was the place to be seen and do business – far more than a place of worship, perhaps a better analogy would be as a freemason lodge, a place for making good contacts and taking part in ritual. It is hardly surprising that, given the leading families of the congregation were involved in the cloth trade, that most chapel members were involved in the wool or cloth trade. The Clarkson family, Gothardts, Scott, Shuttleworth, Aldred, Chambers, Burrell and, much later, the Bakewell families were all wool or cloth merchants, trading or working for either the Milnes, Naylors, or by the 1770s the Lumbs or Holdsworths. Chapel members controlled the vast majority of the cloth trade of Wakefield; indeed, 50 per cent of the cloth trade of Yorkshire passed through the hands of the Milnes family, worth at the time over a million pounds, today many billions.

The town had two water-powered fulling mills for finishing cloth. One was owned by William Hewitt, chapel trustee. Chapel men did not weave cloth, but finished cloth woven elsewhere. The town's two dye works were owned by the Lumbs and Burrells. The Naylors' business was reckoned as controlling one-thirteenth of all cloth produced in the West Riding.

What was so good about the domestic system? The artisans involved could work at their own speed while at home or near their own home, children working in the system were better treated in this system than they were to be in the factory system – as the women of a family usually worked at home, someone was always there to look after the children. Conditions of work were better too as windows could be open, people worked at their own speed and rested when they needed to, meals could be taken when needed, as people worked for themselves they could take a pride in what they did, tension in the workplace was minimal as the family worked as a unit. the best home-produced goods were of a very good quality – though this probably was not true at a general level.

However, the domestic system did have a number of major weaknesses: the production was very slow and the finished product was simply not enough to, in the case of textiles, clothe the fast-growing population of the United Kingdom. A better and faster system of production was needed. the complete process of production was usually done in several cottages and time was lost as materials were taken from cottage to cottage as one stage progressed to the next. the power of water was being developed and small cottages could not possibly take advantage of this source of power. the image of nice quaint country cottages giving workers a quality lifestyle (if not well paid) simply is not a correct one. Defoe witnessed children as young as four working in the domestic system and the waste that gathered around country cottages which did not improve the standard ad quality of life for those who had to live near such waste.

With a growing population that needed feeding, clothing, etc., a new way was needed to meet the demands that a growing population would make on Britain. This would lead to the new factories, large and deep coal mines, huge ship building ports and the growth of our industrial cities with all the problems they were to bring.

WESTGATE CHAPEL AND THE CLOTH TRADE

The mercantile development of Wakefield in the eighteenth century was dominated by Westgate Chapel and the families that worshiped within its walls. Westgate Chapel was the first place of worship built in Wakefield since the Reformation, the sole Unitarian place of worship in the area. The cloth trade had been the life blood of Wakefield since the sixteenth century. It was the place to be seen and do business far more than a place of worship, perhaps a better analogy would be as a freemason lodge – a place for making good contacts and taking part in ritual. It is hardly surprising that, given the leading families were involved in the cloth trade, most chapel members were involved in the wool or cloth trade. The Clarkson family, the Gothardts, Scotts, Shuttleworths, Aldreds and much later the Bakewells, were all wool or cloth merchants, trading or working for either the Milnes, Naylor's, or by the 1770's the Heywood's. Chapel members controlled the vast majority of the cloth trade of Wakefield. The town had two water-powered fulling mills for finishing cloth, one was owned by William Hewitt, chapel trustee. Chapel men did not weave cloth, but finished cloth woven elsewhere. The town's two dye works were owned by the Lumb's and Burrells. The Naylor's business was reckoned as controlling one-thirteenth of all cloth produced in the West Riding.

These men, and some women, dominated the industrial and social economic development of Wakefield throughout the eighteenth and nineteenth centuries.

Thanks to the hard work and industry of these families, most notably Milnes and Naylor's, for Wakefield the thirty-year period from 1780 witnessed a huge expansion of business, and on this new wealth new assembly rooms were built for dancing, the Wakefield Dispensary was founded, the first public library, a free school as well as newspaper. All funded by the profits from the cloth trade. The receipts of the Leeds to Halifax turnpike rose from £852 to £3,500 between 1785 and 1800, and the receipts for the Aire and Calder Navigation tolls trebled from £40,033 a year in 1782 to £150,268 in 1802. In the middle decades of the eighteenth century a second transport revolution took place with the establishment of turnpike trusts in the West Riding as a whole. The promoters of these toll roads promised an alternative system of transport than offered by the canals and navigations. From 1741 Wakefield was linked to the then expanding turnpike network: linked to Halifax via the Wakefield and Weeland turnpike road, Wakefield and Halifax turnpike road and the Doncaster to Halifax road, which also ran through Wakefield and linked the town to the Great North Road, parts of which became turnpike from 1745. The first entirely new route to come directly to Wakefield was in 1789 and was the Wakefield to Aberford road, and replaced a section of the older road from

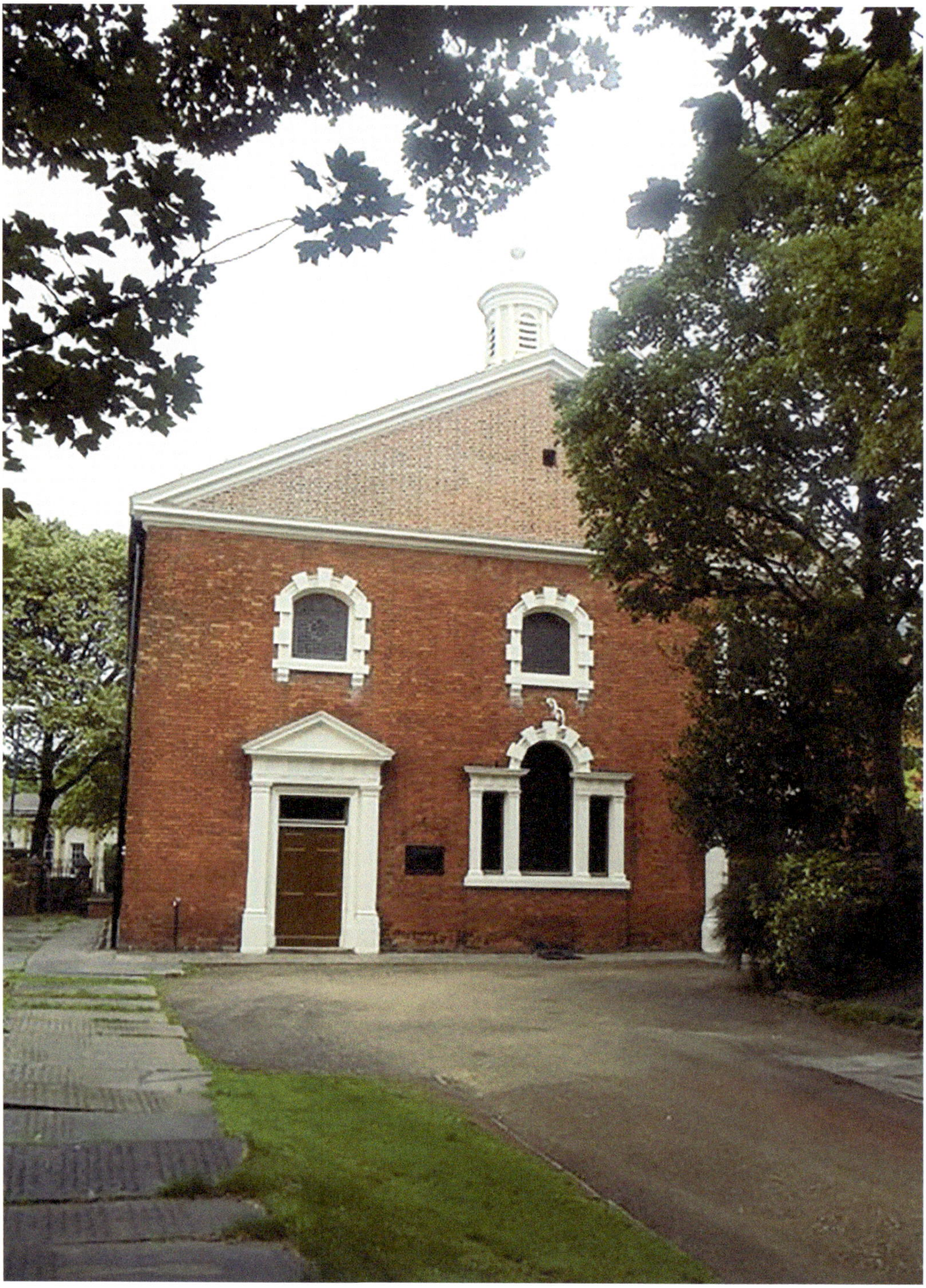

Westgate Chapel, Wakefield. The chapel opened in 1752, replacing an earlier building of 1697. Its congregation dominated the cloth trade in Wakefield for over 200 years.

Wakefield to York. The new road passed mostly across countryside where there had been no previous road. The turnpikes were the motorways of the day.

In 1825 the new Denby Dale road was authorised to be constructed by Act of Parliament, and extended ultimately to Holmfirth, Stalyrbidge and Manchester. To meet the new road on the Ings, Market Street was opened up from the top of Westgate and passed along the side of the cattle market. The road was disturnpiked in 1874. A third turnpike was built, planned to link Kirkgate to Westgate, bypassing the then town centre; work commenced in 1831. In 1863 the road was purchased by the Wakefield Local Board. This road today is Ings Road. In the more modern era the building of the M1 and M62 motorways connected Wakefield to a system of fast, safe and modern roads.

The leading cloth merchants of Wakefield subscribed heavily to both canals and turnpikes. The Milnes family owned considerable stock in the Calder and Hebble Navigation Company and the Weeland Road Turnpike Trust. We know the Milnes use the turnpikes, as in 1768 Pemberton Milnes was returning from market and had his goods on a waggon, which was waiting to pay the toll at Lupset Toll Gate, when it was robbed by highwaymen. The robbers got away with 14 yards of yellow baize. Using the road network was clearly dangerous at times, yet they were a vital transport artery across Yorkshire. In order to improve access to markets, it was common sense for the merchants of Leeds, Wakefield, Huddersfield and Halifax to invest in transport and communication links – it made getting goods to and from markets easier. Yet some historians critique these investments as the merchants should have invested in textile machinery and not roads and canals. The Milnes family managed both, and invested heavily in mechanisation as well as turnpikes and canals. Based on profits from land and the cloth trade, it was Westgate Chapel men who began the industrialisation of the textile industry in Wakefield. Ebenezer Aldred built the first steam-powered mill in Wakefield, followed by Thomas Lumb at Silcoates. Robert Bakewell erected a 'warehouse factory' on Westgate in 1805. The Milnes had mechanised by 1820 – if not earlier. Chapel men also backed a mill at Healey near Ossett. I am indebted to my much-missed friend and co-religionist John Goodchild for his notes on Wakefield mills and the Milnes family.

THE WOOL TRADE

The trade in raw fleece was a major contributor to the economic development of Wakefield since the Middle Ages. The sale of 'fleece off the sheep's back' resulted in the establishment of the raw wool market. The raw wool market was held in Westgate in front of the house that belonged to John Burton, on the site of the modern-day Picture House Cinema. In his will, dated 1753, Burton refers to the house as well as the nearby wool shops and wool market, as well as the tolls and profits arising from the market. Burton was a man of considerable property.

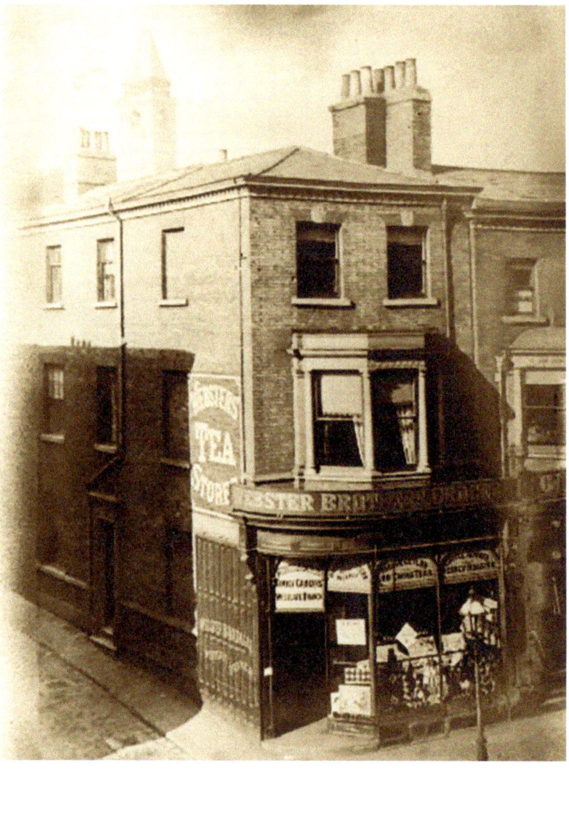

Cheapside *c.* 1880. Cheapside was developed by the Unitarian Soulby family, who were leading wool merchants.

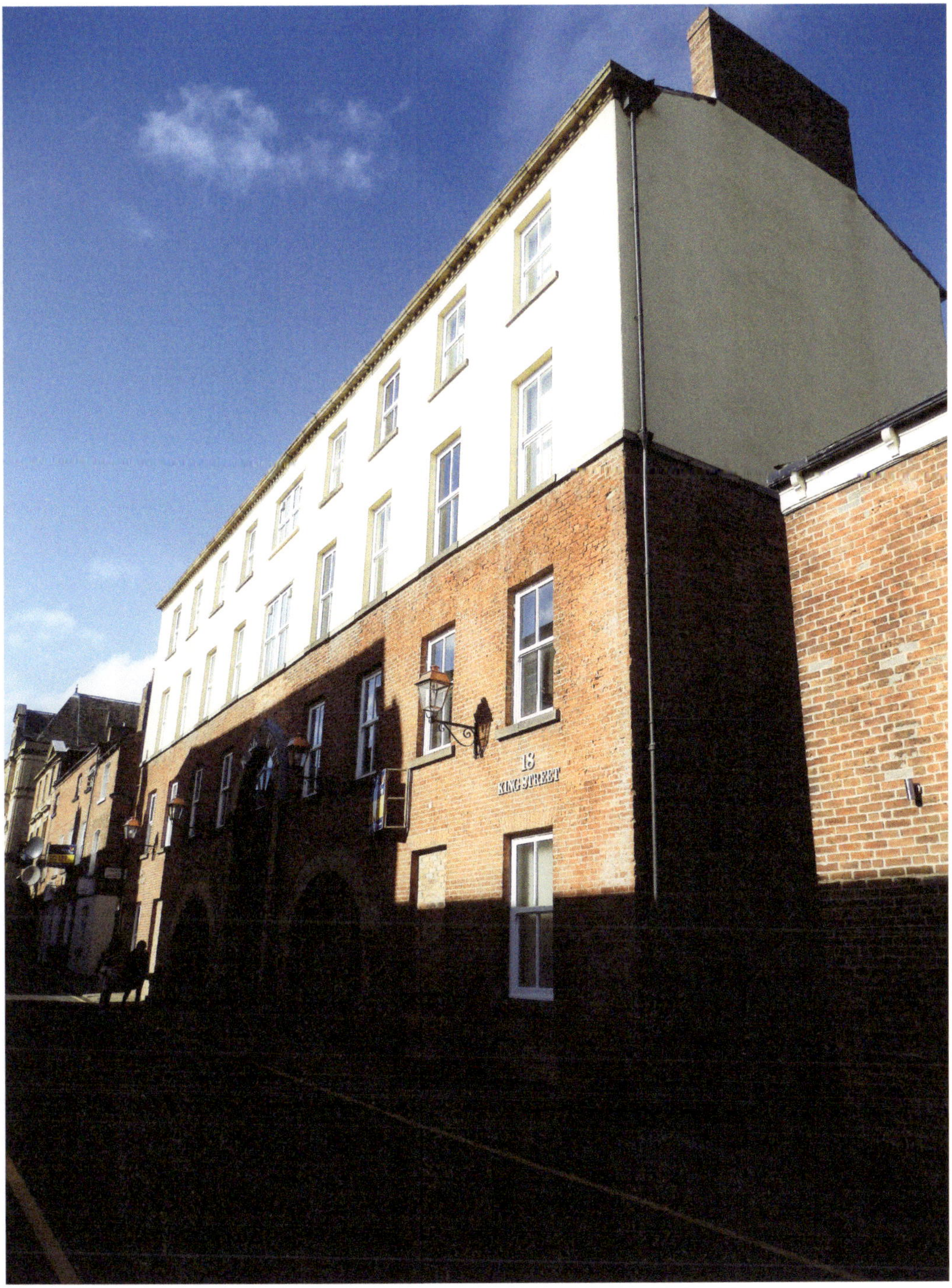

The wool warehouse on King Street where Titus Salt was apprenticed.

Wool-staplers took the fleece to market for sale. John Lumb traded in raw wool in the late seventeenth and early eighteenth centuries, a business his son, also John Lumb, carried on. So successful was he that he was able to build Silcoates House in the 1740s. A diarist records he bought fleeces from Norfolk and Suffolk. He then graded and carded the wool into six or seven different qualities, which he then sold onto spinners.

The Lumbs built a fine mansion on Westgate with warehouses behind. The family business was led latterly by Thomas Lumb (1754–1813). He was the son of John Lumb (1720–1803). In 1782, Thomas Lumb, aged twenty-eight, married a penniless young lady of apparent aristocratic background – Lucy Kendall. He and her father eventually became business partners. They were highly successful wool-staplers and cloth merchants. They had warehouses not only in Wakefield, but also Leeds and Huddersfield. He embraced technology and new ideas, and he erected the third steam-powered mill in Wakefield, at Silcoates. He was also involved with Healey Old Mill Company. The company was managed by five trustees who were responsible for half-yearly shareholder meetings, which were held at the Star Inn, Wakefield. The first chairman was Pemberton Milnes JP, DL (1729–95). In life, Thomas Lumb was a charismatic man of great ability and he took an active part in the affairs of the Wakefield Dispensary and Wakefield Library. In local affairs he subscribed to Westgate Chapel Sunday School from 1785, rebuilt the village school in Alverthorpe, subscribed to Hackney Academy, and backed the Wakefield newspaper the *Wakefield Star* when refounded in 1804. He attended Wakefield theatre and the races. He died on 22 December 1813 aged fifty-nine. His will of 3 July 1812 gave his house, lands and Silcoates Hall to his wife Lucy née Kendall. On her death the estate was to pass to William Kershaw, husband of Hannah Lumb, his uncle Richard's daughter, William Jones Kendall and Daniel Gaskell. He led the radical opposition to the Tories in West Riding election of 1806 and 1807. He had been involved in radical politics since his early twenties, and was a key ally to Jack Milnes the Democrat, the defacto leader of the West Riding radicals for over thirty years.

Another very wealthy wool-stapler was Harper Soulby. It was he who laid out Cheapside in 1806 to provide two spacious houses, one for himself and another for his brother, and developed the road as warehousing for wool-staplers. On King Street, Joseph Jackson built a huge four-floor warehouse to store wool. Titus Salt was an apprentice here.

Others included John Scarth. The Scarth family, Unitarians who attended Westgate Chapel, carried on a business as wool-staplers and wool-factors. The earliest reference to the Scarth business dates from 8 December 1767 when James Scarth, formerly of Wakefield, and John Scarth, late of Thornes, trading as business partners as wool-staplers, dealers and chapmen, were declared bankrupt. Despite this setback, the family continued in business. James's daughter-in-law, Mary, carried on the business and went into business with her brother-in-law Thomas at first and then with John Pollock. The partnership dissolved with Mary's death in 1806.

Once the fleece had been bought from the wool-stapler by the merchant, it needed to be washed, combed and spun into yarn.

WOOL PROCESSING AND SPINNING

In order to process the fleece off the back of the sheep, the fleece had to be washed, carded and combed before it would be spun into fibre. Washing, carding and combing of wool had been done at a domestic level across Yorkshire. By the late eighteenth century, these centuries-old processes done by hand were becoming increasingly mechanised. The first mechanised mill for cleaning and processing the fleece was established in 1781 by Ebenezer Aldred, son of Revd John Aldred, minister of Westgate Chapel until his death in 1760. Aldred also span yarn – it was to be a major industry in Wakefield into the 1980s. Westgate Chapel men had founded what was to become one of the major employers of the city.

ALDRED'S MILL

Revd John Aldred MA, a graduate of Glasgow University, became minister of Westgate Chapel in 1724. He married Mary Naylor, daughter of Wakefield cloth merchant Ebenezer Naylor, and died in 1760 at the age of sixty.

His son Ebenezer Aldred was around fifteen when his father died. In October 1781 Ebenezer purchased land at Westgate Common upon which, by 1783, he had built the first textile mill in the vicinity of Wakefield that was powered by a steam engine – probably a Savery-type engine. 'Aldred engine' is referred to in deeds. Doubts remain as to why the engine was installed. Whether it was a failed attempt to power a mill directly by steam, or due to the lack of flow of water in the Alverthorpe Beck, Aldred modified the mill and installed the engine to assist the wheel. Aldred, in essence, used a steam engine as a pump to draw water to turn the wheel. The mill was insured in 1786 and when it was mortgaged in May 1787 it was described as 'lately erected … for the purpose of Scribbling and Carding wool and Frizing of cloth'. In terms of machinery, the mill possessed 'one double carding engine, five other carding engines, one very large carding engine, all covered with good cards and in good repair; two carding engines uncovered with cards, one-wheel cylinder, three billies, one willy, two jennies and various other articles'.

What were these machines? The first process was to break the fleece up. The fleece was beaten to remove dirt and opened using a willy or woolley mill. The mill had one of these. The next stage involved carding the fleece.

Carding is a mechanical process that disentangles, cleans and intermixes fibres to produce a continuous web or sliver suitable for subsequent processing. This is achieved by passing the fibres between differentially moving surfaces covered with card clothing. It breaks up locks and unorganised clumps of fibre and then aligns the individual fibres to be parallel with each other. When preparing wool fibre for spinning, carding is the step that comes after teasing. With woollen, two carding machines were used: the first, or the scribbler, opened and mixed the fibres; the second, or the condenser, mixed and formed the web. The mill had nine carding engines. We assume the scribbling machines were listed in the other items of machinery, as the mill is specifically described as 'scribbling'. The mill had a 'Slubbing Billy'. This was a machine for putting a twist into freshly carded wool so that it can be spun. It was used to process partly spun wool or 'rovings' from the piecing machine into a leaner yarn, which could then be spun. The mill also had two jennies. We can be sure that Aldred was spinning yarn. He does not seem to have dyed the fleece or yarn. The finished yarn was then sold to clothiers, who had it woven into cloth. The finished cloth came back to the mill to be fulled.

Aldred became a partner in the Healey New Mill Company in 1785, which was very much a Westgate Chapel venture. In December 1791 Ebenezer left the Healey partnership and took with him some of the now dated machinery from Healey to his own scribbling mill. Aldred faced fiscal issues in 1793 and co-religionist James Milnes stepped in with a loan secured against the property for £1,000 at 5 per cent interest. Aldred went bust in 1795 and a commission was opened against him in November when it was said he was liable to be sent to gaol. When the mill was sold early in 1795 the newly built premises included a house occupied by the Aldred family, 'the Stock-house, Warehouse, Engine-house, Fire engine, Outhouses, Garden on the east side of Westgate Common commanding the entire and continual Stream of Water of Westgate Common Beck … the whole purposely constructed

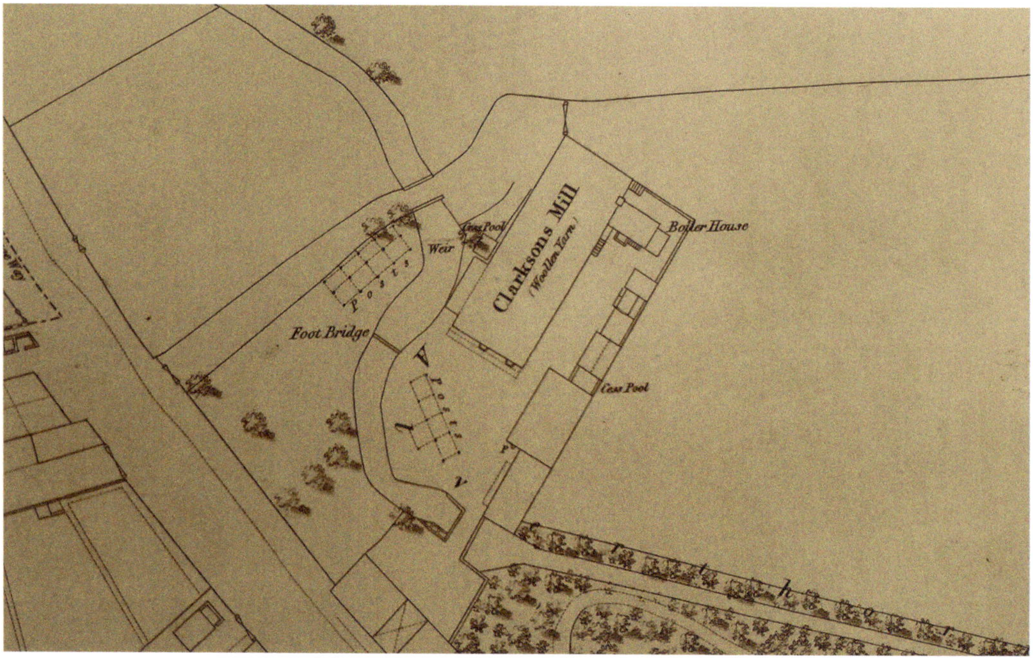

Aldred's Mill on Westgate Common became owned by the Clarkson family from 1796. By 1900 it was known as Alfred Haley and Company.

and, in all Respects, well calculated for carrying on the Business of Scribbling, Carding & Spinning Wool'.

The mill was bought by Aldred's co-religionist John Clarkson, and the mill continued in operation under new owners, the Clarkson family, all Westgate Chapel people, well into the nineteenth century. Indeed, in 1834 John Clarkson, secretary to the chapel trustees, was employing twenty-seven males and eight females. In the nineteenth century it became Haley's Mill.

HOLDSWORTH MILL

Wakefield's second scribbling and spinning mill was in operation by 1790. As with Aldred, the Holdsworths attended Westgate Chapel. Samuel and Joseph Holdsworth bought land at Westgate End in 1788. It was here that they built a new mill. The Holdsworth families had been associated firstly with the dissenters' chapel at Westgate End. Stephen Holdsworth (1705–63) was superintendent during the building of the current Westgate Chapel, which replaced the chapel at Westgate End. Stephen had married Hannah, the sister of Nathaniel Hulme MD, FRS, FSA. Her father, Revd Samuel Hulme was a leading Protestant dissenter.

In 1798, Murray, Fenton and Wood of Leeds installed a steam engine to power the mill complex owned by Messrs S. and J. Holdsworth. They are listed in 1785 as spinners and manufacturers – we can be certain that, as with Aldred, the Holdsworths were processing raw fleece into yarn. Indeed, members of the family were wool-staplers. The co-partnership was dissolved in 1813. The mill became the property of Thomas Marriott.

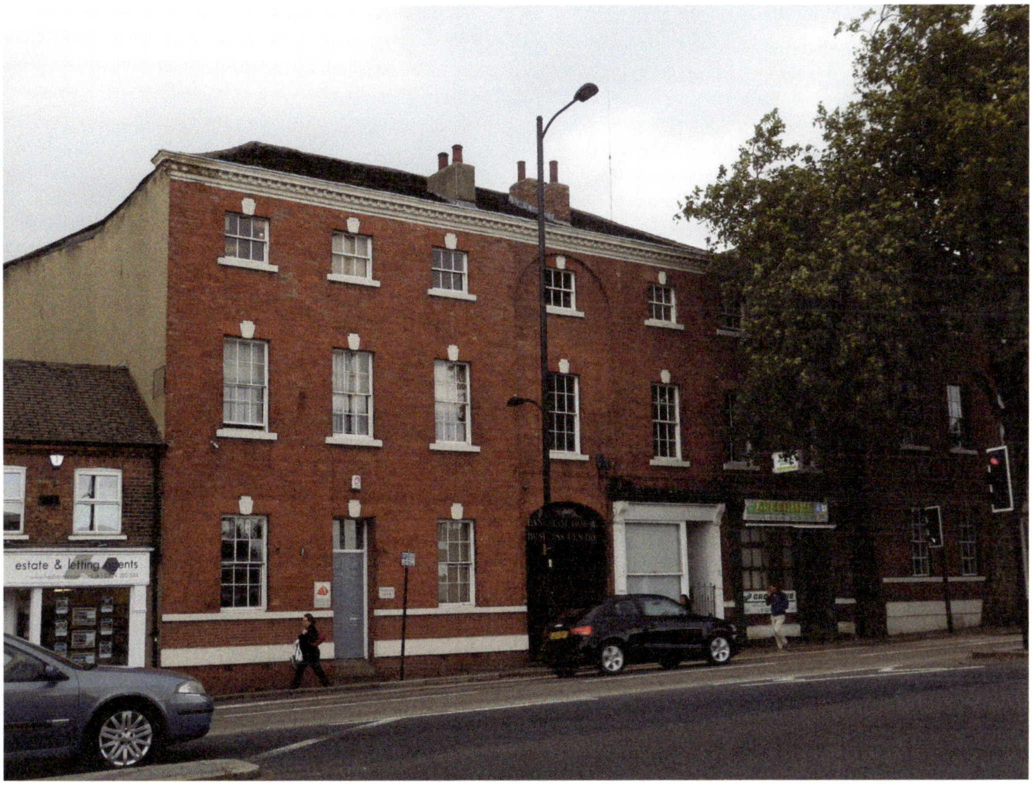

The Westgate home of the Holdsworth family, leading cloth merchants and mill owners.

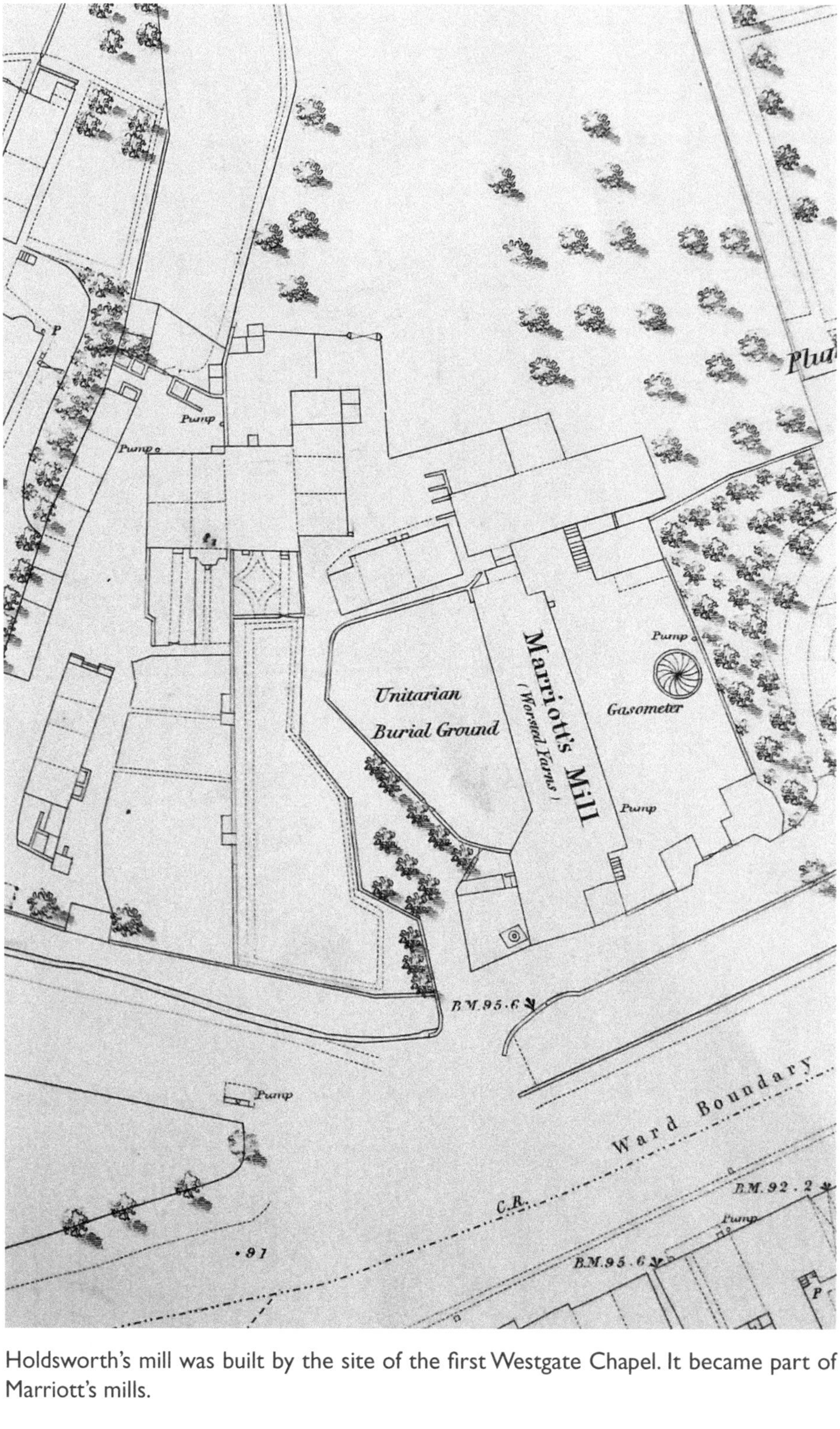

Holdsworth's mill was built by the site of the first Westgate Chapel. It became part of Marriott's mills.

HEBBLE MILL

Thomas Wood Sr was baptised at Westgate Chapel on 7 September 1762, son of Benjamin Wood. Thomas's daughter Sarah married her co-religionist and neighbour Benjamin Clarkson of Alverthorpe Hall, parents of Clara Maria Clarkson.

Sometime in 1785 he purchased 5 acres of land and buildings in Flanshaw for £410. He was a master handloom weaver, the son of a clothier. He was literate, and many letters between him and his daughter survive in the John Goodchild collection. By 1790 he had prospered sufficiently as a weaver and clothier to build a large and new fulling mill on his land at Flanshaw, powered by a steam engine provided by Fall Ing Foundry, Wakefield. The mill commenced operation in October or November 1791 and was known as Hebble Mill. The mill was performing the functions of processing the raw wool, cleaning it and straightening (scribbling), as well as fulling the finished woven cloth.

The business was not successful at first, so in 1796 Thomas sold a three-quarter share to John Cooke of Swinton. The opening of Smithson's tramway alongside the mill provided a cheap and convenient supply of coal for the mill. Wood continued in control of the mill until his death in 1817; he was buried in the yard of Westgate Chapel. Under the terms of his will the mill passed to his son Benjamin, who had married Ann Barff. The Barffs managed a large Wakefield wool-stapling company. From 1828 William Marriott, a Westgate Chapel man, was tenant of the mill until 1837. It was destroyed by fire in 1905 and comprehensively rebuilt. Today the business is known as Sirdar.

SILCOATES MILL

The Lumb family were dyers and wool-staplers. They bought fleece, graded and processed. To do so they had a fleece-breaking yard and warehouse on Westgate, and in 1794 built a steam-powered mill at Silcoates to card, scribble, wash, spin and dye yarn. Thomas Lumb died in 1813. The mill passed to his nephew who leased the mill to Messrs Robinson & Dawson, yarn spinners from 1834, for an annual rent of £160. The mill was enlarged in 1836–37 – the same year it was mortgaged for £4,253. In 1850 the mill was leased to George Conyers of Ossett for fourteen years at £240 a year. The lease was renewed in 1864 to Mr Ellis of Ossett for fourteen years at £210 a year. John Crossley bought the mill in 1871. By the turn of the twentieth century Silcoates Mill was trading as Lister and Glover. By now it was described as 'rag merchants and mungo manufacturers'. Lister and Glover's partnership was dissolved on 31 December 1902 and the mill seems to have closed down shortly afterwards. The mill remained disused for thirty years, not being demolished until 1936. The site of the recreation ground at the bottom of Silcoates Lane is where the mill once stood.

THORNES LANE MILL

The mill was insured in 1796 and is listed as a 'steam powered woollen mill', with the owner being Jonathan Chambers. It had been newly built in that year. The engine was supplied by Benjamin Aydon and John Elwell of Fall Ings Foundry. The mill stood on the corner of Thornes Lane and Thornes Wharf Lane and was connected to Smithson's Tramway, which provided coal for engines from Haigh Moor Colliery. Unsurprisingly, Chambers married his co-religionist Priscilla Burrell. The marriage was blessed with several children: Jonathan (baptised 19 August 1780), Joseph (baptised 28 April 1782) and Richard baptised (5 June 1784). The Burrells were

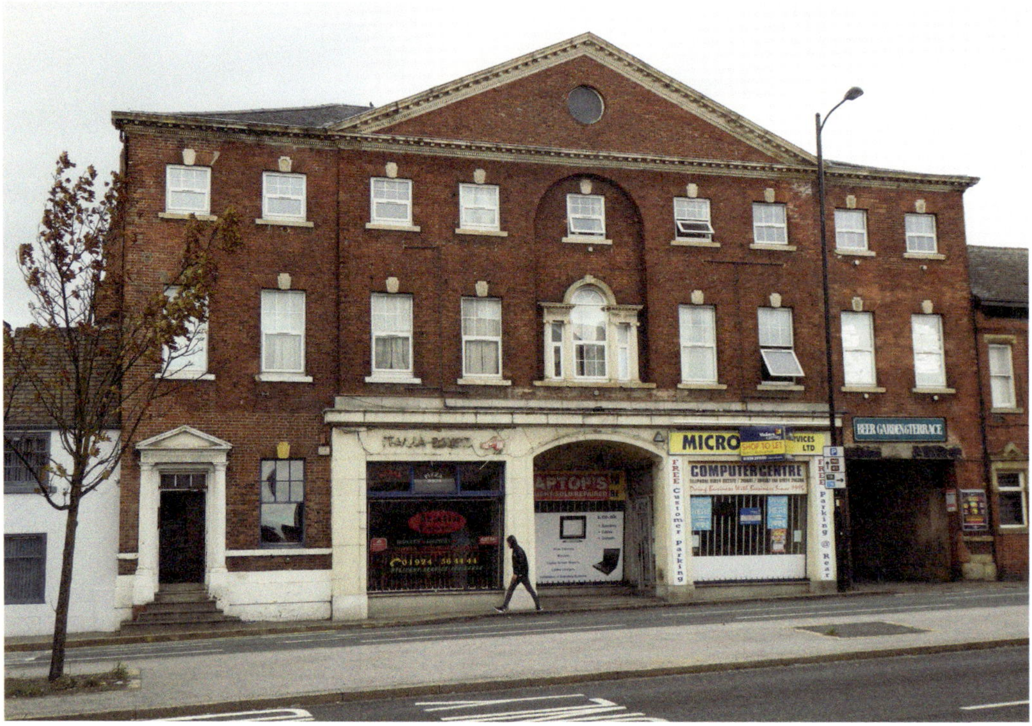

The magnificent Westgate mansion of Robert Lumb, a wool merchant and leading member of Westgate Chapel. His nephew, Thomas Lumb, built Silcoates Mill; his father had built Silcoates House.

lifelong Unitarians for many generations as were the Chambers family. Priscilla was the widow of William Burrell, who had founded Burrell's dye works, and had found herself a single mother to four. The marriage was one of convenience, we suspect, as Chambers' factory directly adjoined the Burrells dye works – through marriage the Chambers gained free access to a dye works for their processed yarn! The mill was insured again in 1800 for £1,500. Thornes Lane Mill was an early example of a complete factory system, whereby raw fleece was cleaned and processed into yarn, woven into fabric, dyed and finished. The dye works and mill closed in 1824.

FLANSHAW MILL

Flanshaw Mill completed in 1808 was built by Thomas Ward and Thomas Waite, the mill was steam powered as is described as 'Flanshaw Factory' in a document of June 1808. By 1815, part of the mill, the steam engine, three scribbling machines and three carding machines and warehouses were let to Thomas Marriott. In 1834 this part of the mill was let to William Holdsworth- who upon for closing of his lease of Bank Lane Mill with Rachel Milnes at Back Lane Milnes, needed new, smaller and cheaper premises. He used new smaller premises to finish cloth. He set up five gig mills, six brushing mills, six shearing frames and other machinery. Holdsworth like Marriott were Unitarians. October 1841 the entire mill complex was let to Benjamin Oakes, the family being members of Zion congregational church. William Oakes built Flanshaw Congregational Church in 1866 and is buried in the grounds of the church. The mill closed in 1927.

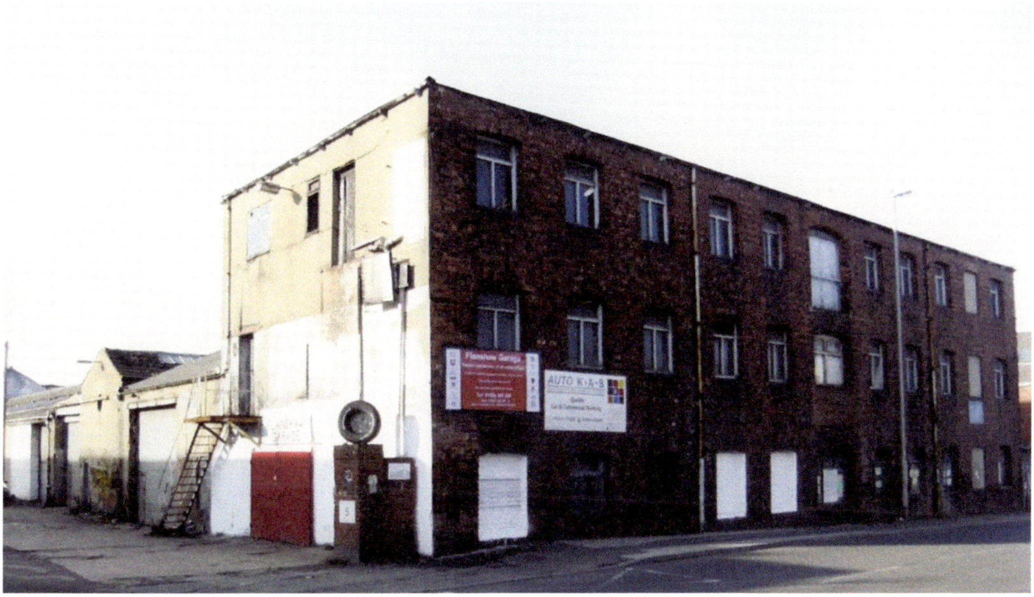

Above and below: Flanshaw Mill was established in 1808 by the Ward family. It was taken over by Thomas Marriott soon after and became Oakes Mill in the middle years of the nineteenth century. It closed in 1927.

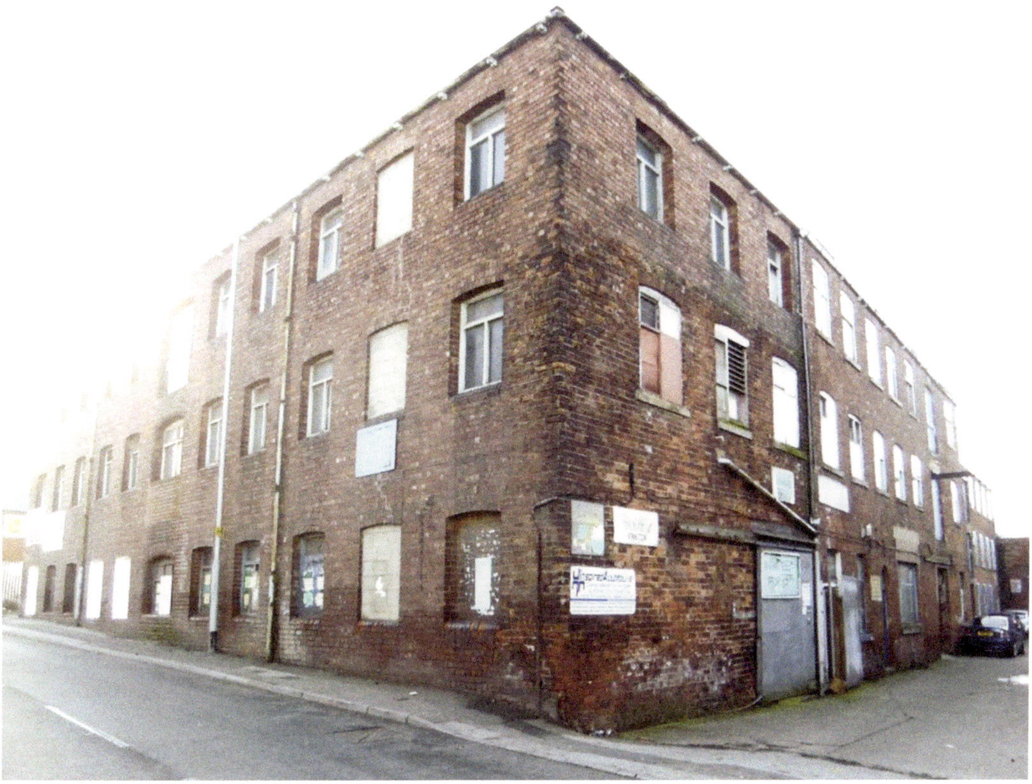

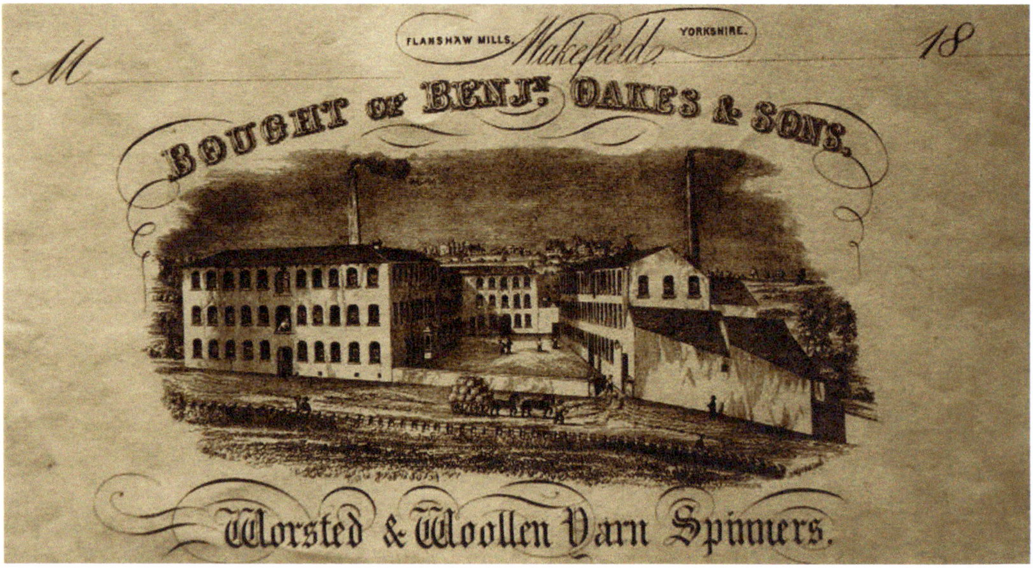

Bill of sale for William Oakes & Sons of Flanshaw Mill.

MARRIOTT'S MILL

Thomas Marriott (1761–1832) first appears in Wakefield around 1800. In 1803 he had set up premises next door to Milnes, Heywood & Co.- was there a link between the two firms beyond being Unitarians and Westgate Chapel members? In 1815 he took on Flanshaw Mill, which had opened in 1808. He leased the premises for yarn spinning. He leased the steam engine, three scribbling machines and three carding engines for £280 a year for a ten-year period. In 1820 he and his son William leased the Tammy Hall and converted it into a worsted mill, managed by James Micklethwaite, whose daughter had married his son William Marriott. So successful was Thomas Marriot as a worsted spinner that he took over the failing Hebble Mill from co-religionists in the 1820s, and on land on Westgate, bought from the Holdsworths between 1822 and 1823, he erected Plumpton Park. This was a huge purpose-built mill, complete with a large mansion house. When William Marriott died on 8 February 1832 aged forty-two the business being passed to his wife. Under her guidance the mill at Westgate End was enlarged in 1837, and the takeover of Balne Milne from the bankrupt Tottenham Lee began. Balne Mill later became owned by the Holdsworth family.

Thomas's grandson, William Thomas, took over the running of the concern in the 1850s. A disagreement with his brother Alfred witnessed the closure of the Westgate End mill in 1871, but business carried on at Balne Mill. The Westgate End mill stood derelict until the very end of the nineteenth century, when it was demolished and the current terrace, called 'Plumpton', was built. In the 1850s and 1860s Marriott's business was the most prosperous and largest business in Wakefield. His business interest witnessed the purchase of Wrenthorpe Colliery He prospered so much in 1867 he purchased Sandal Grange for the then immense sum of £15,059 8s. Marriott also had interested in Newton Colliery at Snow Hill and Wrenthorpe Colliery. In 1892 Wrenthorpe Colliery had to close for eleven weeks to repair the machinery. Rather than let his workers go with no pay, he paid all his workers' wages for eleven weeks from his own personal funds. He gave during his lifetime vast sums to the establishment of

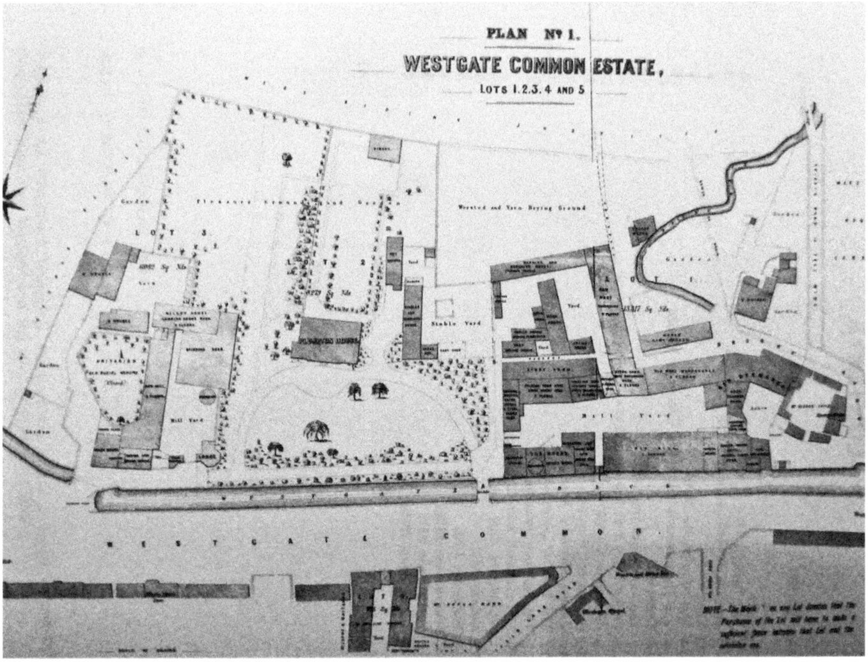

Map of the vast mill complex on Westgate Common owned by the Marriott family.

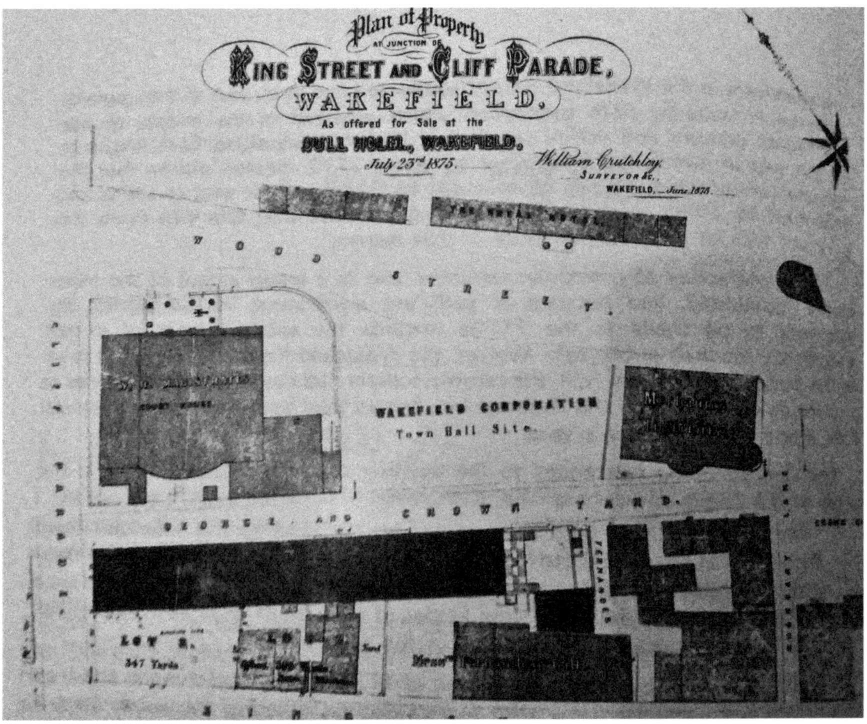

For a time the Tammy Hall was a worsted mill owned by Thomas Marriott. This map shows the scale of the building before it was partly demolished to make way for the Town Hall.

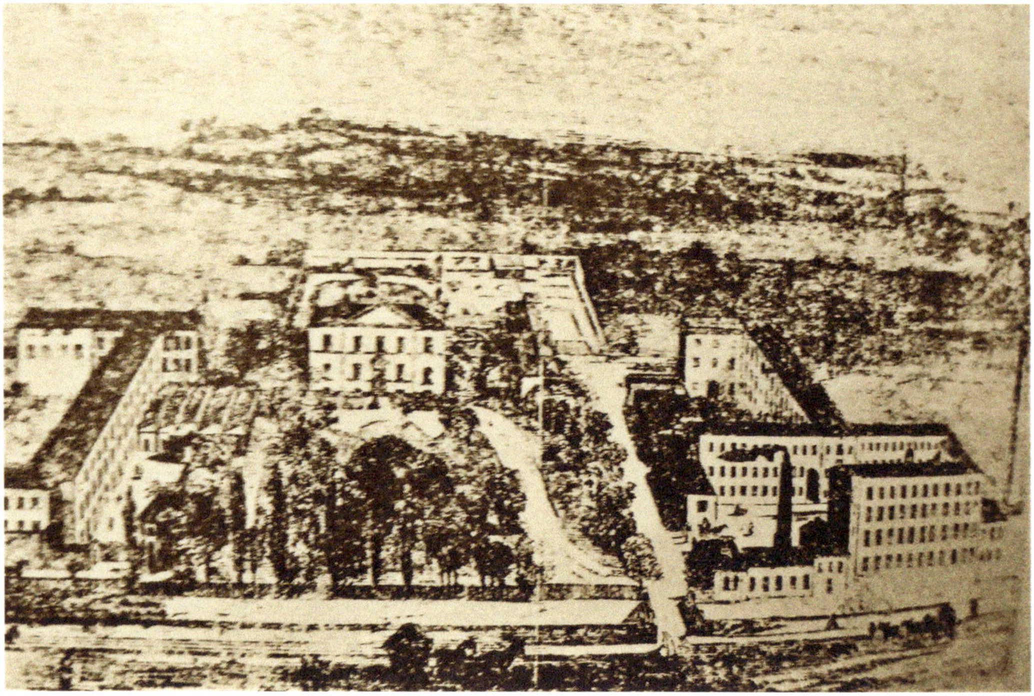

A rare engraving of Marriott's Mill on Westgate – it was a vast industrial complex.

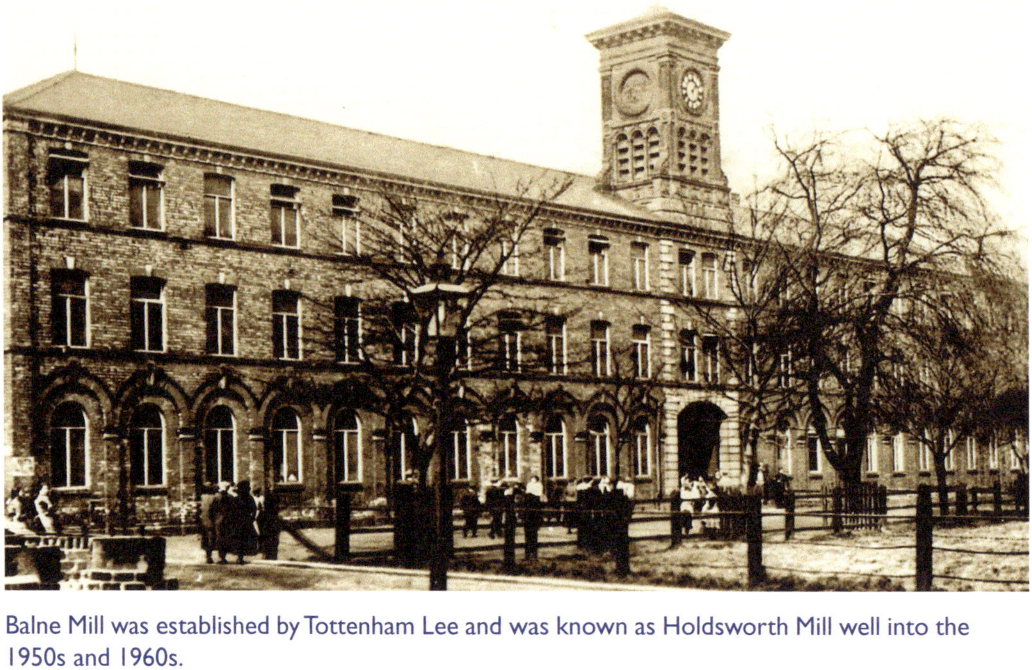

Balne Mill was established by Tottenham Lee and was known as Holdsworth Mill well into the 1950s and 1960s.

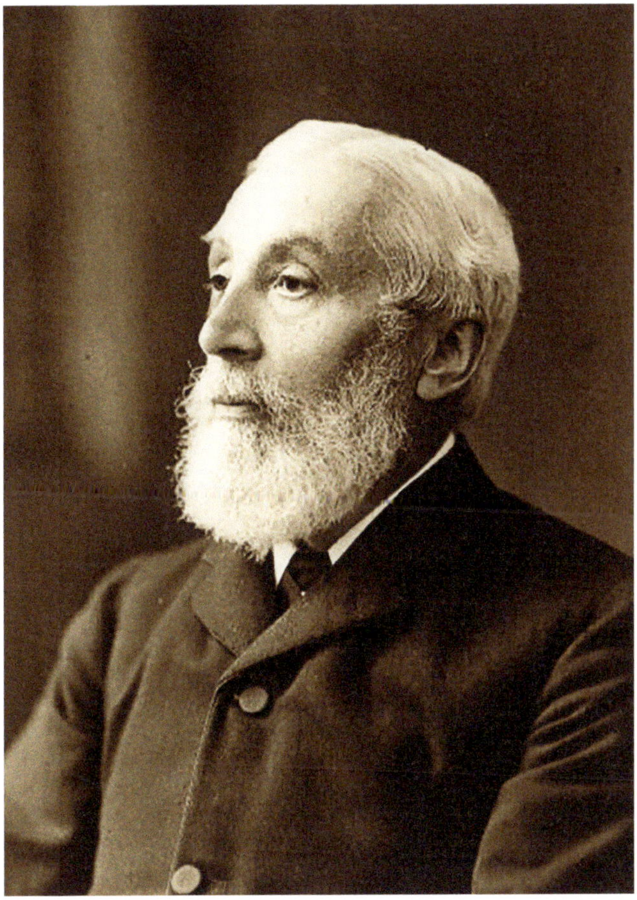

William Thomas Marriott, lifelong Unitarian and philanthropist.

Clarence Park and the rebuilding of Clayton Hospital, for the establishment of the Yorkshire College, which is today University of Leeds.

He and his wife, like his parents before him and grandfather, were lifelong Unitarians and active members of Westgate Chapel. He died in 1899 and is buried in the chapel yard, next to his parents' graves. As a mark of respect, the bells of the cathedral tolled throughout his funeral service at Westgate Chapel. His daughter marred Revd Andrew Chalmers and his son carried on the spinning business until 1910. Mrs Marriott died in 1920 and is buried with her husband in the chapel yard.

OTHER BUSINESSES

James Milnes financed Thornes Fulling Mill, which was completed in 1804. It became later Paton & Baldwins. Two more steam powered mills appeared by 1805: Robert Bakewell opened on Westgate Common a 'warehouse factory'. Daniel Washington, was a cloth merchant and member of Westgate Chapel, like Bakewell. He established a joint stock mill in Wakefield in 1805. Thanks to huge investment by Westgate Chapel men, by 1815 there were ten steam-powered mills in Wakefield. Expansion was slow and steady; by 1838 Wakefield had thirteen steam-powered mills, totalling 240 horse power employing 916 people per mill

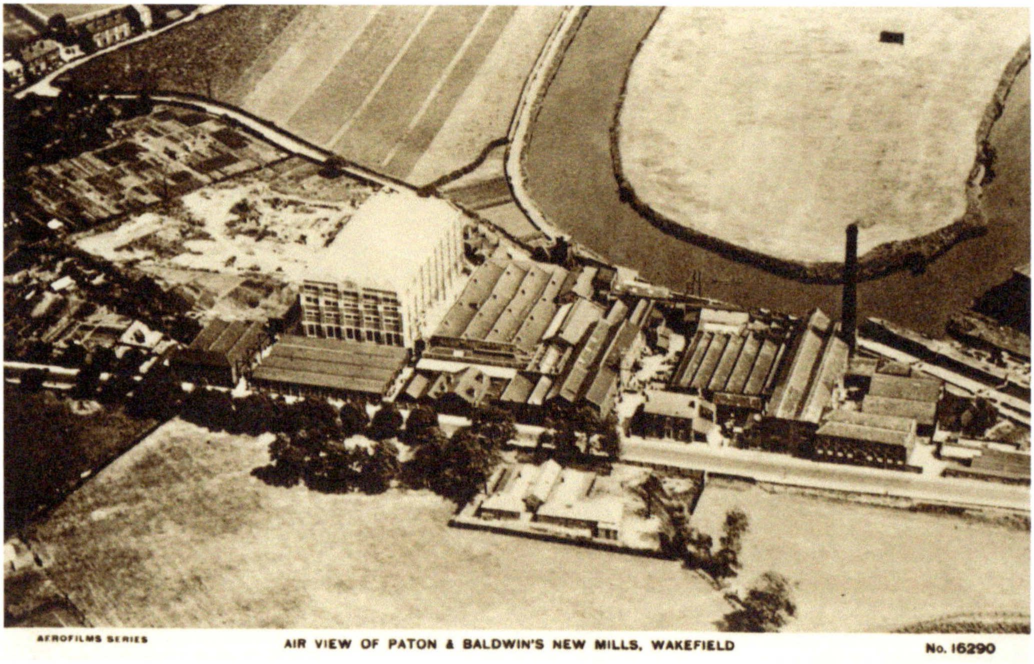

Aerial photograph of the large complex of Paton and Baldwins on Denby Dale road. The site was cleared in the 1980s to make way for light industrial units.

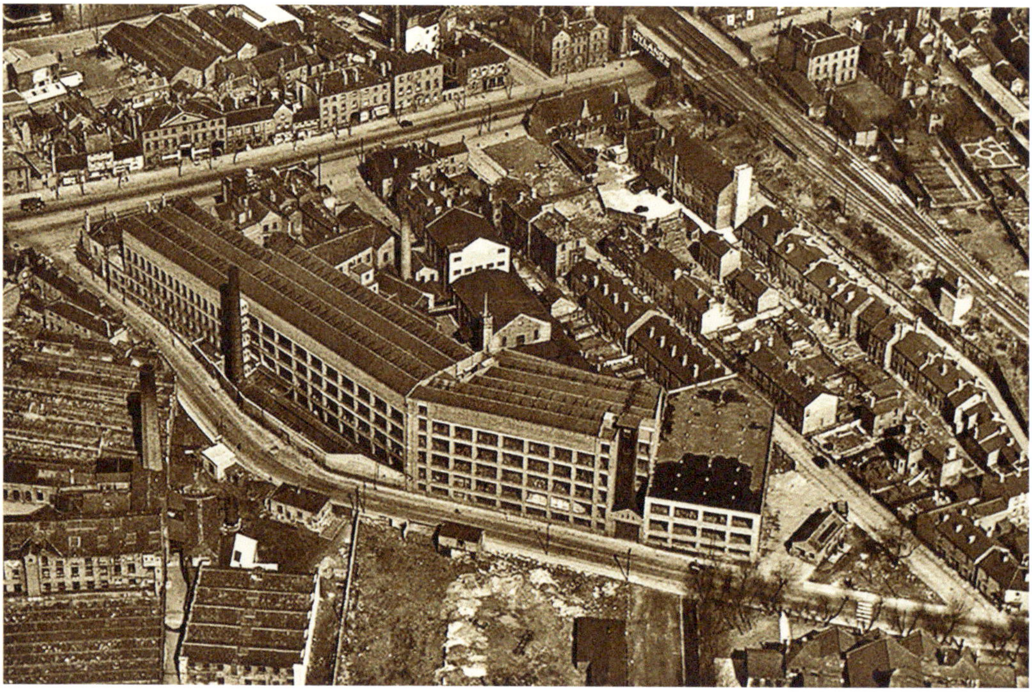

Aerial photograph of the vast complex of MP Stonehouses that stood on the junction of Ings Road and Westgate until *c.* 1990, when it was swept away for retail units.

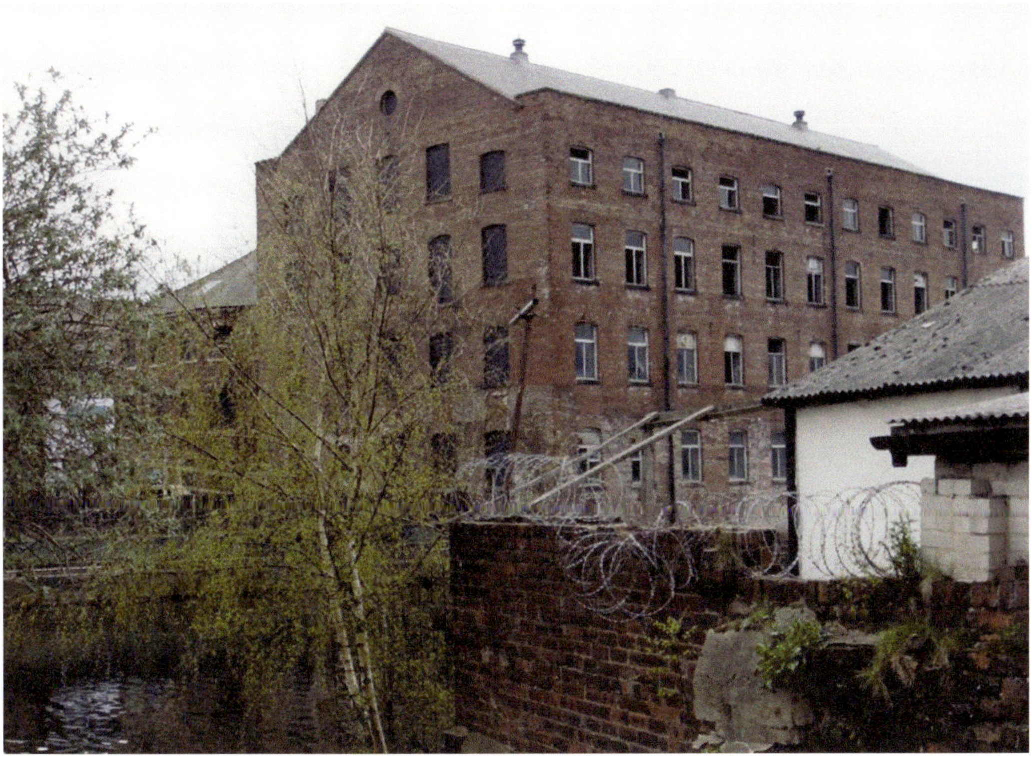

Above, below and next page: The Rutland Mill complex, which lays on the bank of the River Calder. It was built between 1872 and 1875 by Isaac Briggs, a retired railway contractor. It is the last remaining mill complex in Wakefield and deserves to be preserved to keep the city's proud textile heritage alive.

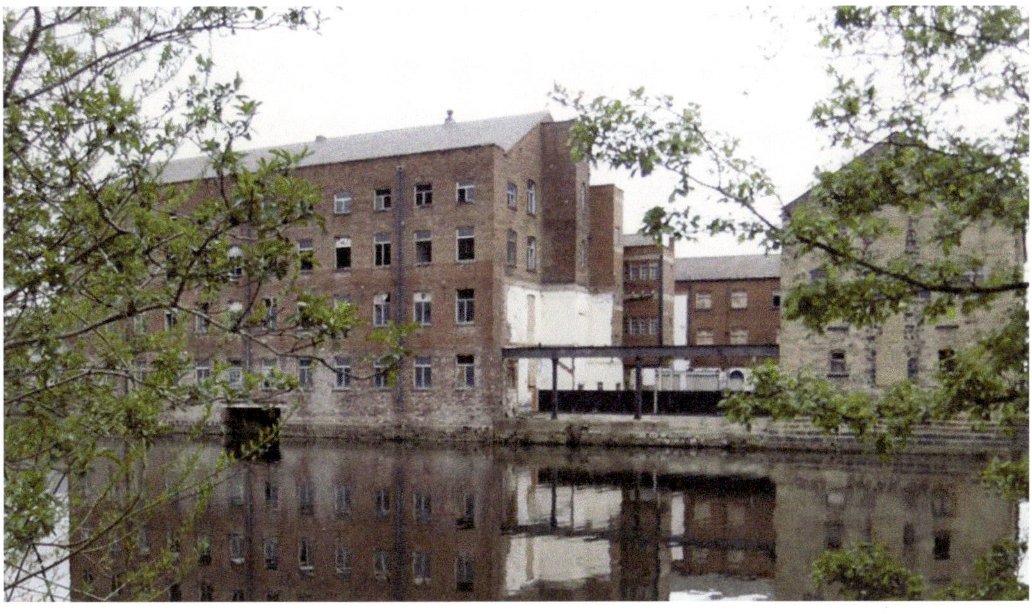

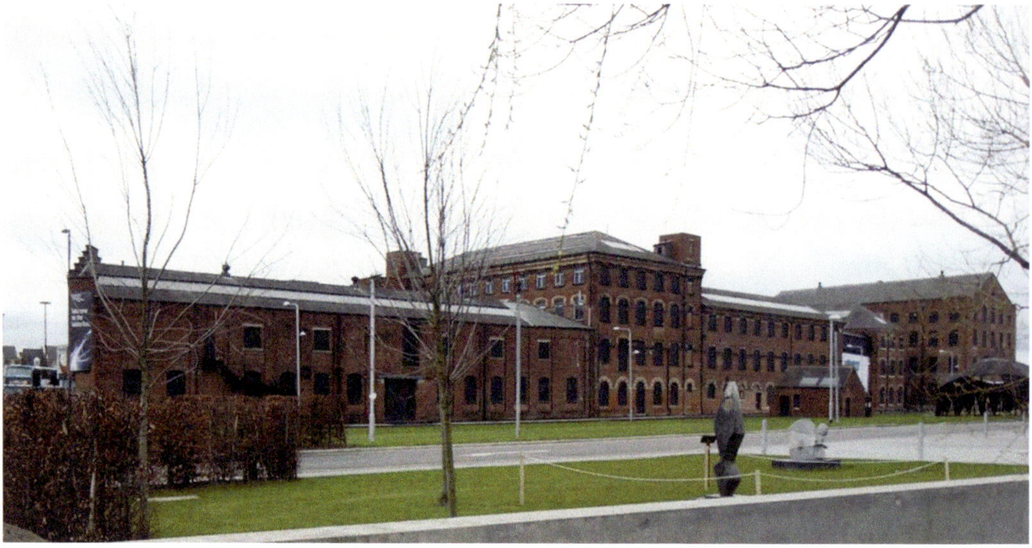

and in 1850 there were seventeen mills, with 34,167 spindles and 1,195 staff. In addition, was a single mill which was both spinning and weaving cloth with 480 spindles and 163 looms employing 14 men and 168 women. The concerns of Marriott, and later Barker [later Paten and Baldwin] became important business in the town. Many can still remember M P Stonehouse's vast premises on Ings Road. In 1913 Baldwin and Partners had 18,000 spindles at Rutland and Thornes Mill, Alfred Haley & Co at Westgate Common had 20,000 spindles, as did Holdsworth & Co on Balne Lane, George Lee & Sons at Providence Mills had 10,000 and Stonehouse's a modest 8,000.

CLOTH PRODUCTION

Since the fourteenth century, handloom weaving had been the primary mode of production of any cloth. The West Riding weavers' cottages, with their wide mullioned windows, let light into the workshop. The men and women who made the cloth were known as clothiers. They bought the finished yard and wove it into cloth. Before spinning was mechanised, the combing, carding and spinning of yarn was carried out by the clothier. The Shuttleworth family of Outwood, later of Wakefield, is one of the few clothier families we have names for. Their handlooms were situated in Shuttleworth's Yard, which was swept away in the 1860s to build Westgate railway station. The Shuttleworths were the principal cloth makers to the Milnes family and attended Westgate Chapel.

The weaving process for wool did not mechanise at the same rate as for cotton. Despite ten mills producing spun yarn by 1815, only one mill was producing machine-made cloth – Back Lane Mill.

BACK LANE MILL

By 1785, there is evidence that the Milnes family were manufacturing cloth, and by 1794 they had built Wakefield's first modern mill and Wakefield's first factory. It stood on Westgate on a site now partially under Westgate railway station. The firm had been founded in the early eighteenth century by Richard Milnes and it was managed by his sons – John, Robert and Pemberton. With the death of John and Robert Milnes, co-partners in Milnes & Co. in 1771, the firm continued as Pem & John Milnes & Co.

In 1774, Pem & John Milnes became trustees and investors in Halifax Piece Hall, which opened in 1779, and also the Leeds White Cloth Hall. In 1775 the surviving partner, Pemberton Milnes, took in the business his nephew John Milnes, aka 'Jack Milnes the Democrat', and Arthur and Benjamin Heywood and formed Milnes, Heywood & Co. Into this venture, Pemberton invested £30,000, Jack invested £20,000, and Arthur and Benjamin Heywood invested £10,000 each. Jack was the driving force behind the concern, which in 1783 controlled over 50 per cent of the cloth trade of the West Riding. Jack left the business in 1794 when he mortgaged his share for £7,000 to his uncle. Pemberton Milnes died in 1795 and his share of the business was passed under the terms of his will to Richard Slater Milnes MP, the son of his brother Robert.

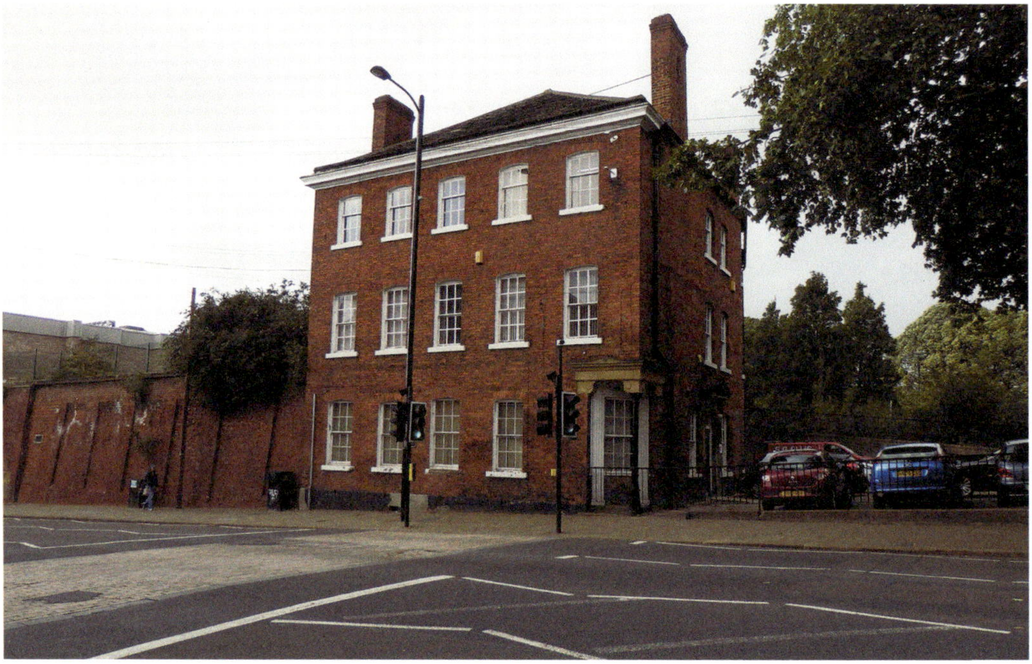

Pemberton House – one of the last remaining mansions built by the Milnes family on Westgate. It was built by Pemberton Milnes in 1757–58, who was a leading, if not *the* leading, Nonconformist politician and cloth magnate of the eighteenth century in the north of England. He lies in the catacombs beneath Westgate Chapel with his wife Jane and daughter Mary Bridgette, Duchess Galway.

Richard Slater Milnes died in 1804 and management of Milnes, Heywood & Co. passed to his widow Rachel Milnes. It was she who managed the company for many decades. In order to bring capital into the concern, in 1806 she entered into partnership with Thomas and William Holdsworth, trading as cloth merchants under the name Milnes, Heywood & Holdsworth & Co. The mill was insured in 1823 for £7,400, when George Lee is listed as occupier and or manager of the mill. George Lee was baptised at Westgate Chapel and went on to found George Lee & Sons, owner of Providence Mill on Westgate.

On 6 October 1824 the partnership of Milnes, Heywood & Holdsworth was dissolved and Rachel took up the reins of running the business again. A few years later, the mill was leased for eight years in September 1827 to William Holdsworth for a yearly rent of £1,525. The mill was over five floors, and the weaving shop was over three floors. The mill was described thusly:

In the Mill

Ground Floor: four gigs with scrays and one teazle brush, pieces oven, iron press with threaded screws, one hundred and fifty-three cast iron plates, sixteen dozen and a half fencing, one hundred and ninety-two dozen pressing papers, one boiler for raising steam. One wet brushing mill.

First floor: two double scribblers, two double carders, two billeys, one willey, four mules containing 967 spindles, two jennies.

Second Floor: one double scribbler, one billey, eight shear boards and frames, four patent shearing frames, two brushing mills, one new double carder.

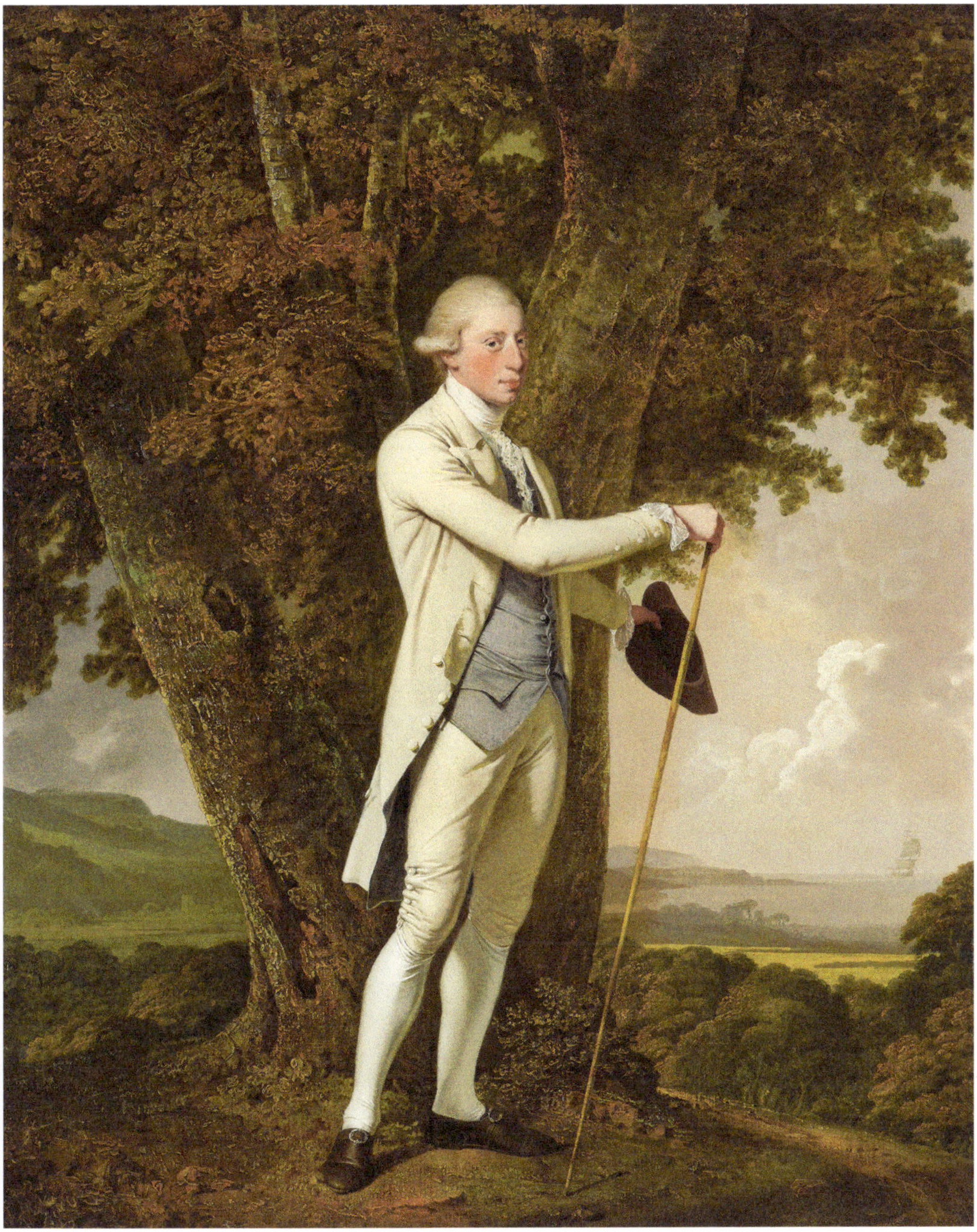

John Milnes (1751–1810) leading cloth merchant and radical left-wing politician. He lies beneath Westgate Chapel, along with his father, also John, wife Catherine and daughter Caroline.

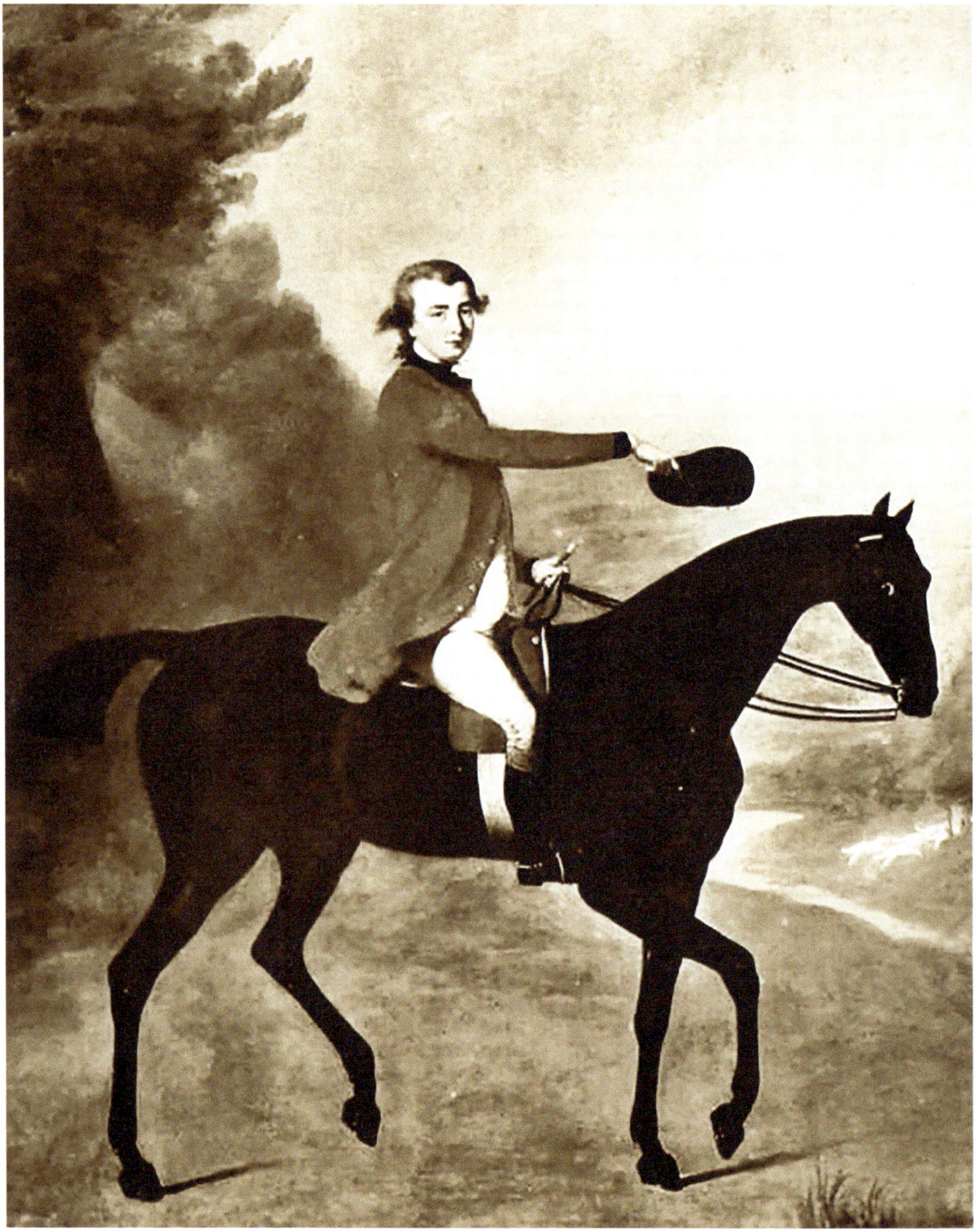

Richard Slate Milnes, Member of Parliament for the city of York from 1784 to 1802, was a friend of William Wilberforce and the radical politician Revd Christopher Wyville. He died in 1804 and lies buried beneath Westgate Chapel, not far from the grave of his father Robert Milnes, his mother Joyce and stepmother Esther.

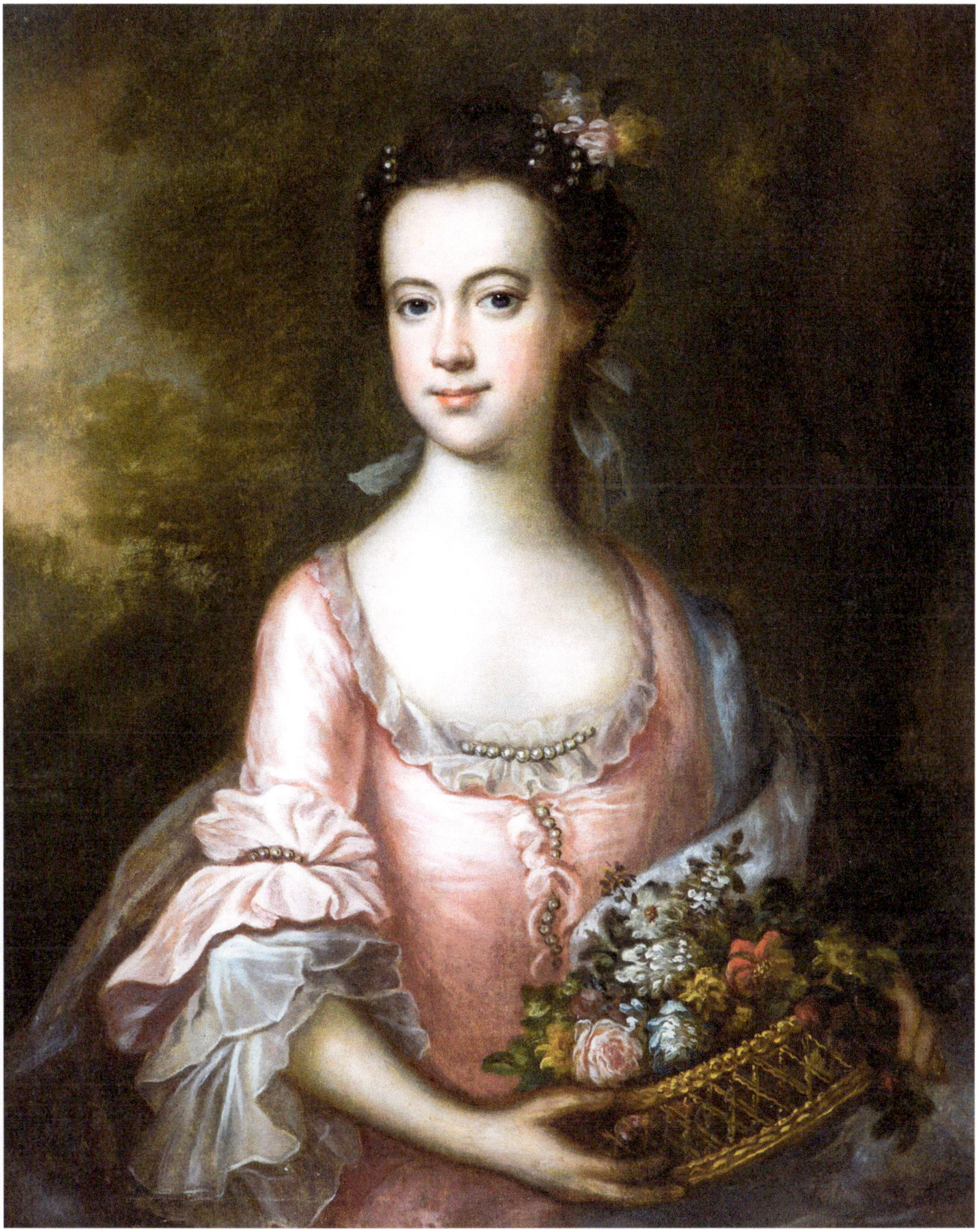

Rachel Milnes, the second daughter of Hans Busck, leading cloth merchant of Leeds and trustee of Call Lane Unitarian Chapel. Rachel was a skilled and adept businesswoman. Her elder sister, Mary Anne, married James Milnes MP, nephew of her husband Richard Slater Milnes.

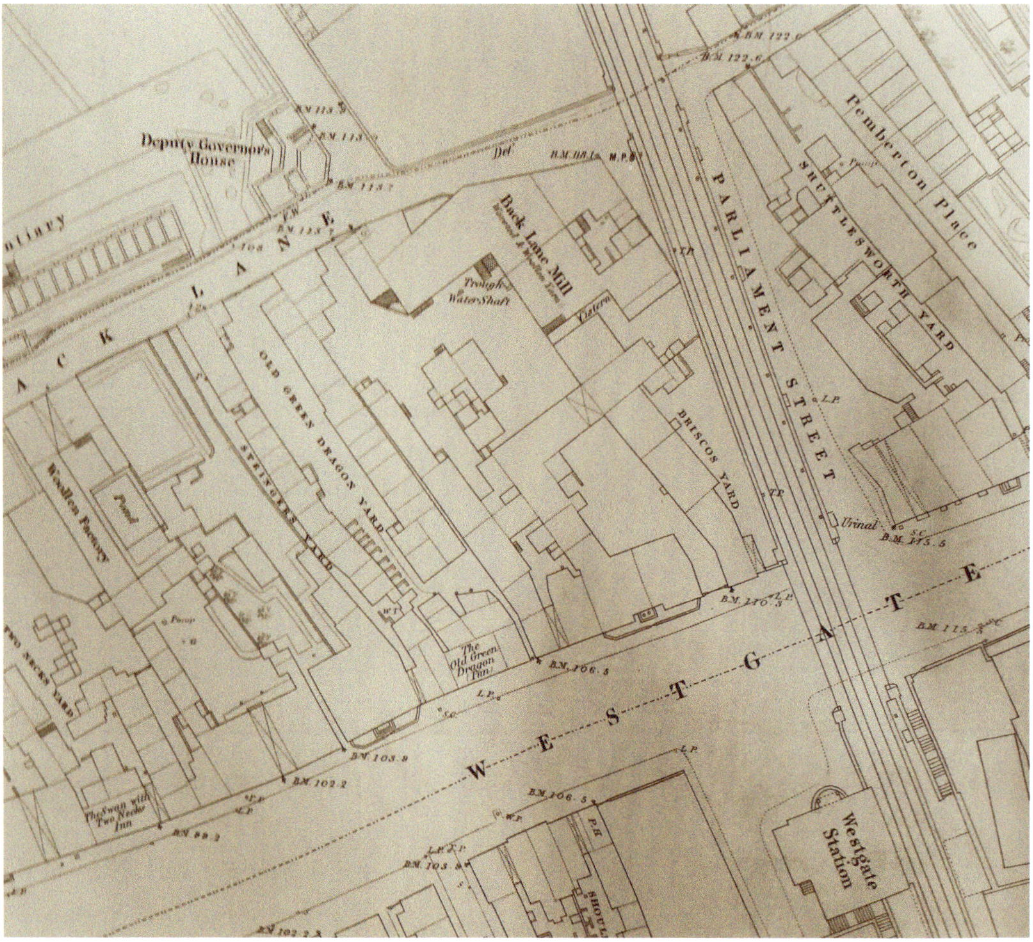

In the centre of the image we see Back Lane Mill, the first purpose-built mechanised textile factory in Wakefield, which was managed by Rachel Milnes from 1804 to 1831. Nothing of this mill complex exists in modern Wakefield.

Third Floor: three double scribblers, three double carders, three billeys, one willey, one birling, one brushing mill.
Attic. Three jennys, five burling tables.

Weaving Shop
Ground Floor: three bar trees, crutcher and one iron stove.
First Floor: seven broad looms.
Second Floor Seven broad looms.

Narrow Weaving Shop
Five narrow looms and one iron stove.

Water for the steam engine, dye shop and fulling stocks came from a reservoir behind the mill, on the Love Lane, and now lies buried under the former Prison Training College. The reservoir is shown on the enclosure map of 1794, which suggests the engine was erected by this date. The water travelled underground to the boiler house and then flowed into the main sewer that ran along Westgate. From the list of machines it is clear that this was the first factory in Wakefield for cloth production. Raw fleece went into the mill and finished cloth came out, either as broadcloth or worsted. The first stage was the processing of the fleece. In the second stage, the mill span the fibres into yarn, having four mules with 967 spindles and an additional five jennies for spinning. The jennies were man powered; the mules would have been powered by the steam engine. The use of jennies and mules reveals different quality of yarn was being produced – mules were used for finer yarn. It was no doubt made using the Saxon fleece that the family imported from Germany – they had been making superfine fabrics since the 1770s.

After producing the yarn, it was then sent to the weaving shop to be placed on either one of the fourteen broad looms or five narrow looms. The narrow looms are likely to have made worsted and superfine fabrics for the Huddersfield market and exports. As soon as it had been woven the cloth was ready for the 'mill'. The cloth was examined for defects in the burling chamber – the attic of the mill. The cloth was then put into the stocks, which was no doubt steam powered. The first phase involved cleaning and scouring the cloth. The mill, described as a fulling mill, would have had a large tank with a flow of water, into which the cloth was soaked before being put under the hammers of the stocks. The cloth was then dried at a tenter ground (likely on the other side of Back Lane – land owned by the family since the 1720s). At this stage the cloth would normally be sold by the clothier to the merchant to have the cloth finished; indeed, this is what made the Milnes family its fortune.

Not so in the new factory. By the end of the eighteenth century new technology was rapidly replacing the tried and tested hand finishing and cropping of cloth. The Milnes factory boasted a mechanised finishing process. The mill had four gig mills and twelve shearing boards. Gig mills for the raising broad cloths had been in use in Huddersfield since 1791, and the use in Wakefield predated that of Leeds by a decade. Gig mills in Wakefield are mentioned in the committee report on the wool trade of 1806, as are mechanical shearing frames. The gig mills and shearing frames would have been powered by the steam engine. The mill had two types of shearing frames: one the type of 1787, and the second the patent type introduced in 1794. How the mill avoided the Luddites in 1812 is not known. Clarkson's Mill was threatened but not attacked. But history says nothing about Back Lane Mill in this episode.

William Holdsworth went bankrupt in 1829 and gave up his tenancy of the mill to take over part of Flanshaw Mill where he erected five gig mills, six brushing mills, six shearing frames and other equipment to finish cloth. Rachel Milnes found herself running the mill once more. Under her tenure a second, new, larger boiler was installed in 1829. Due to large gambling debts run up by her second son, Richard Rodes Milnes, Rachel sold the family business and home (Fryston Hall) to pay off his creditors, and the mill was bought in 1832 by John Scott and Samuel Clay. The sale included Langham House, the Holdsworth family home on Westgate with worsted factory behind, warehouses on Garden Street and also the Black Horse public house. It should be no surprise that the mill was sold to co-religionists.

Scott and Clay ran the mill for a decade until it was sold in November 1842, by which time the mill possessed a 12-hp condensing steam engine with two boilers, six power looms, thirteen winding engines with thirty spindles and other machinery. It was demolished to make way for Westgate railway station in 1866.

It should not be a surprise that the Milnes had a factory system by the 1790s. Benjamin Hallas, a Methodist from Ossett, developed an early steam-powered blanket making factory. Cloth was dyed at Pildacre Mill as early as 1793, and in 1795 machinery at the mill included two forty-spindle jennies, a twenty-six-spindle billey, a number of power looms, a carding engine and a scribbling machine. A new steam engine was bought for the mill. A very serious fire in 1814 burned Pildacre Mill to the ground, at a total loss of over £10,000. The mill was rebuilt, then closed finally in the 1960s before being demolished in the 1970s.

OTHER BUSINESSES

Cloth production in Wakefield rapidly expanded in the middle decades of the nineteenth century. In the 1860s the Colbeck brothers built Alverthorpe Mill, latterly known as Matthew Walker Ltd. By 1887 the mill was producing cloth for the army, navy and police force and had 180 power looms. The mill concern lasted until recent years.

Other cloth manufacturers were Joseph Wade & son of Portobello Mill, which opened in 1861. The mill was built in the late 1830s as a worsted spinning mill by Joseph Holdsworth of Belle Isle dye works. The mill was powered by a 50-hp steam engine and a smaller 30-hp engine. It was taken over by Henry Currer Briggs and Walter Shepherd – Westgate Chapel men – as a cocoa matting manufacture between 1846 and 1861. The mill was later bought by Joseph Wade. By 1878 the mill had ninety-one looms and had 300 employees; by 1913 101 looms are listed, and in 1919 there are 103. The firm went bust in 1955 and the premises became home to the Wakefield Shirt Company. George and James Stubley erected Calder Mills in the 1870s, which had 300 looms in operation in 1919 and survived until around 1936.

On the opposite bank of the river stood Castlebank Mills, built by Joseph Booth. Little is known about the business, other than the premises were built in 1869 and it had 300 looms at its peak. The firm went bust in 1936. The mill is still involved in textile production as W. E. Rawson.

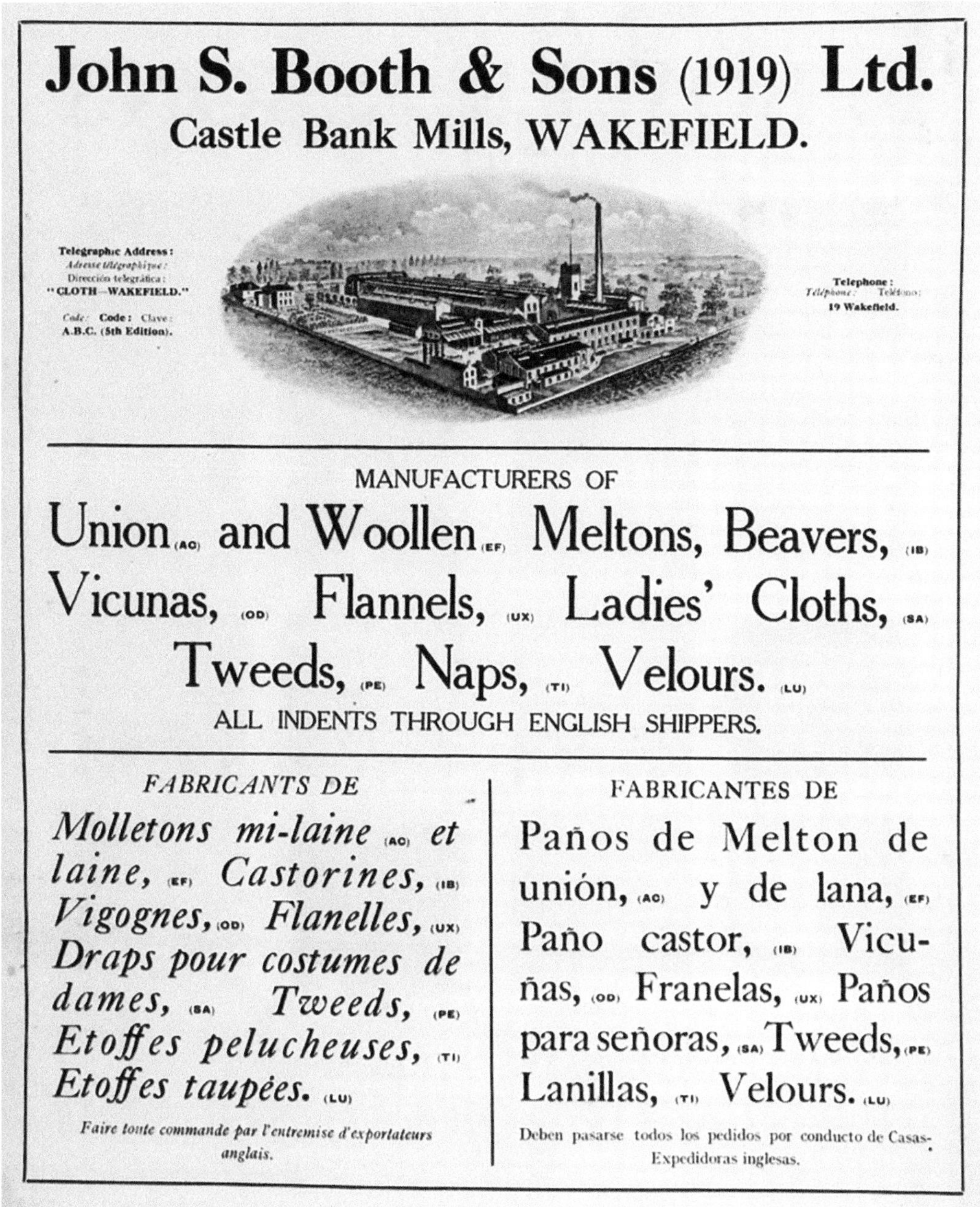

Advertisement for Castlebank Mills. Castlebank Mills was built by Joseph Booth in 1869 and at its peak had 300 looms. It went bust in 1936.

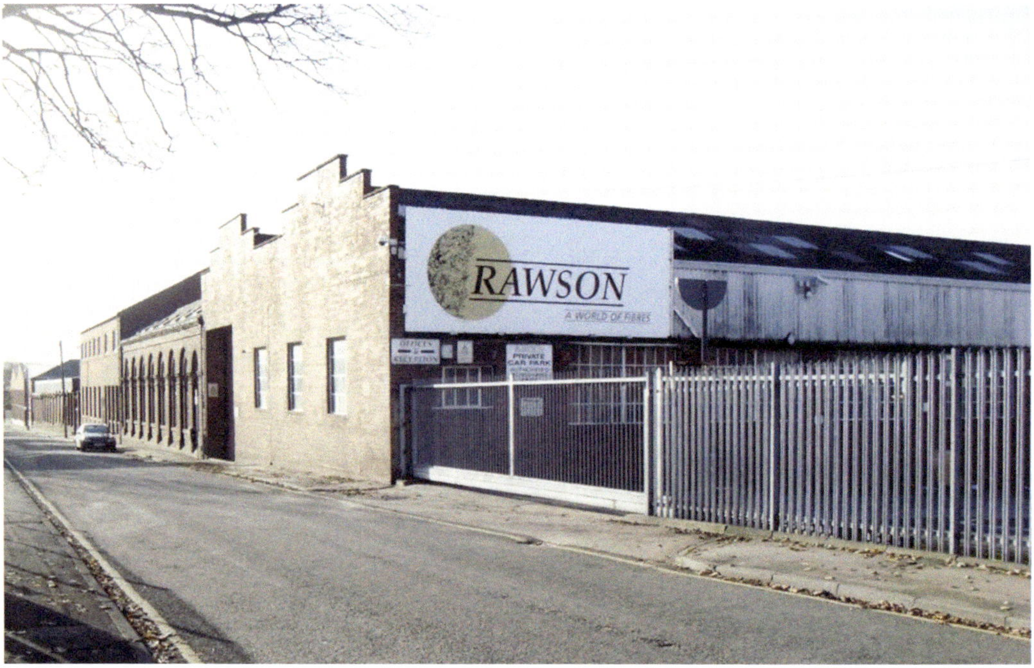

Castlebank Mills is still involved with textile production as Rawsons.

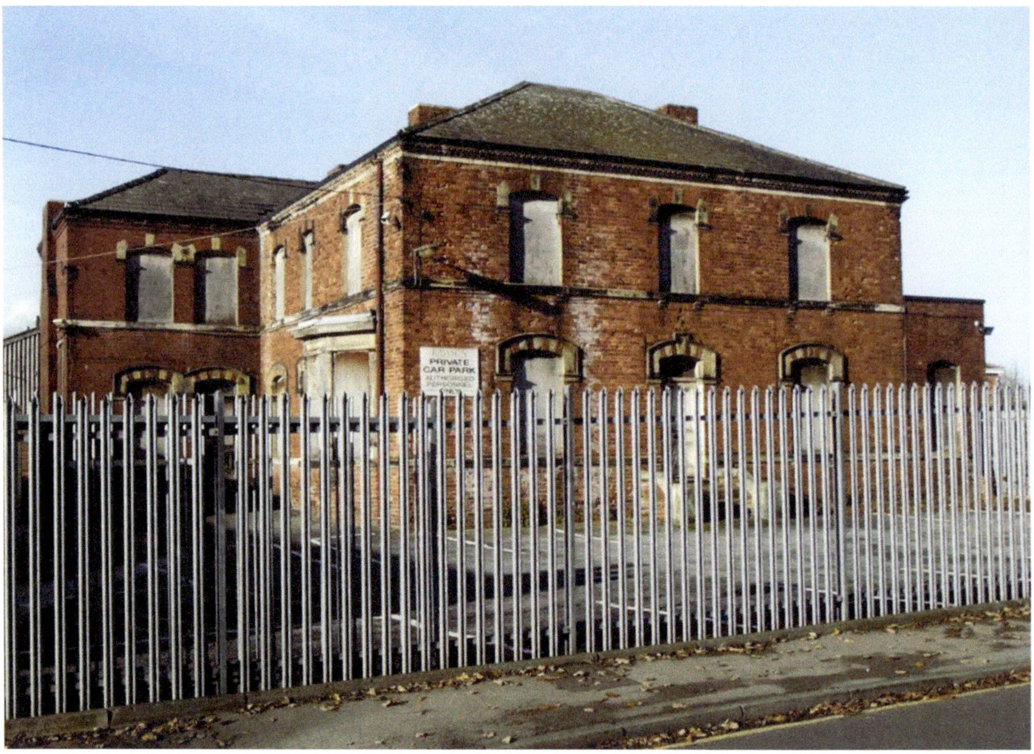

The now derelict offices of Joseph Booth & Sons at Castlebank Mills.

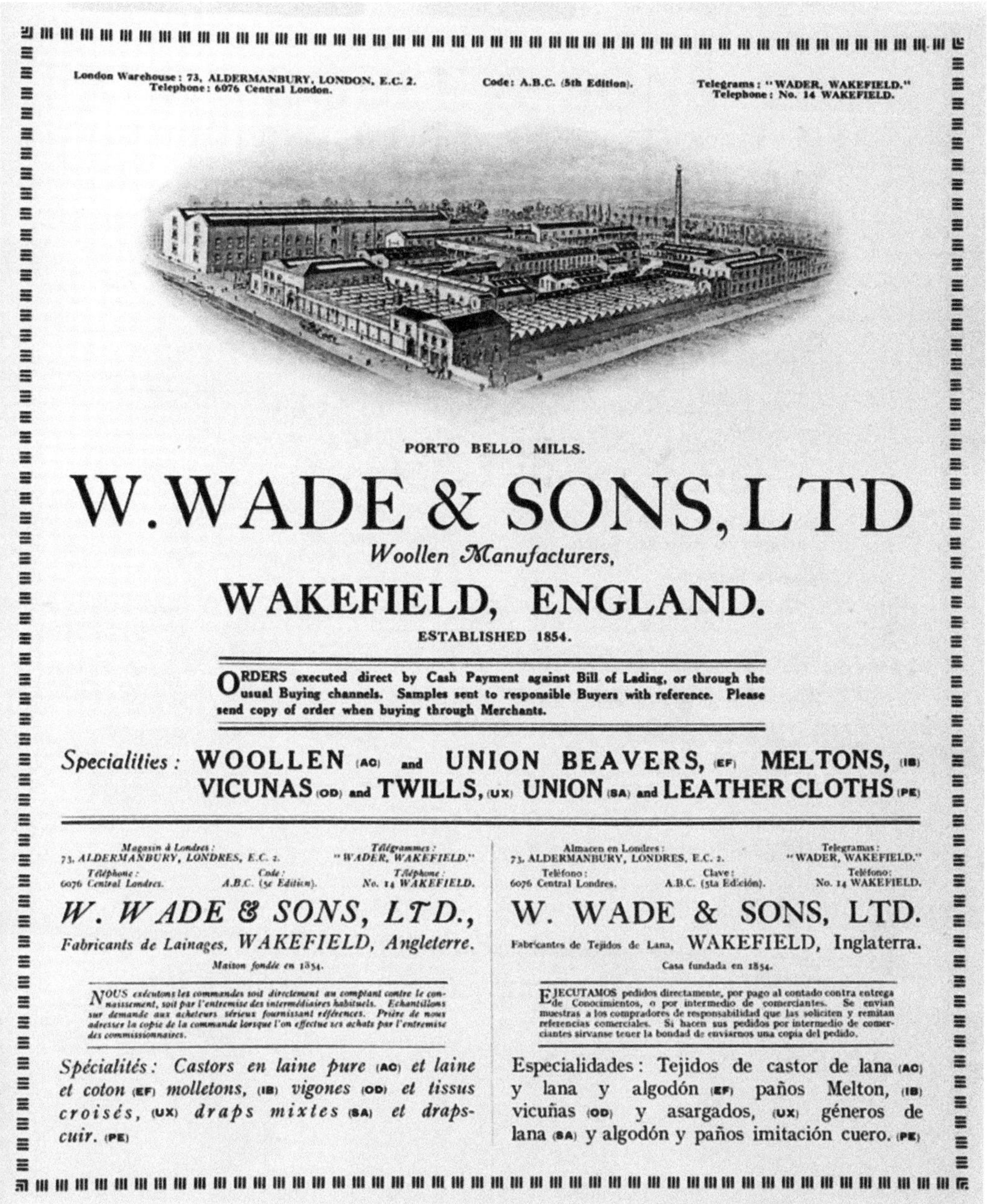

Advert for Wade & Sons at Portobello Mills. The firm went bust in 1955 and the premises became home to the Wakefield Shirt Company.

CLOTH MERCHANTS

Once the cloth had been woven on the loom, it had to be finished. In the eighteenth century, as for centuries before, this was done by hand with shears. Master cloth dressers were skilled men. The leading dressers in Wakefield were the Scott family, who lived in Scott's Yard, Westgate. The increasing mechanisation of cloth dressing with gig mills and shearing frames resulted in the Luddite riots of 1811 and 1812. By 1800, the Milnes family had erected Gig Mills to finish cloth by 1800, and sometime later so too did John Clarkson at Westgate Common Mill. In 1819 J&J Naylor had erected a steam engine to power both fulling stocks, gig mills and shearing frames. William Holdsworth took over Flanshaw Mill to finish cloth in 1831 – again using gig mills.

The finishing process for cloth included raising the nap of the cloth with teasels or similar, fulling the cloth, dying the cloth and pressing the cloth. Huge profits could be made by buying cloth off the loom and finishing it. The Milnes family had done this since the 1680s, as had co-religionists the Naylors. Naylors' premises were demolished to make way for a retail park in the 1990s. The finished cloth was packed into bales and taken for sale at Leeds Coloured Cloth Hall, Halifax Piece Hall or Huddersfield Cloth Hall, or was exported. Huge profits were made from buying unfinished cloth, dyeing it, finishing the cloth and selling it on. Since the 1690s, the Milnes' fortune was based on the cloth trade; indeed, Jack Milnes believed that the family business purchased over 50 per cent of all white cloth produced in the county. They were trading into Russia, as well as to America. They were also importing cotton as back cargo. They made huge profits from the trade and an eighteenth-century diarist tells:

> Mr Mills Wakefield Merchant trades into all parts, has into Germany Spain, Lisbon, Italy, Holland and all parts of Russia besides country trade has to London and Bristol and to a deal of seaports besides.' and continues 'Wakefield, Mr Mills, Richard and John and Pemberton all 3 partners sends a deal of bale goods from Wakefield to Manchester so the take shipping and goes down to Liverpool (and to Bristol) then are boarded of a ship of theire own wich sayles into the East and West Indias.

Indeed, the Milnes had the monopoly of supplying cloth to the Russian army. They also imported cotton from the Netherlands and from markets in Hamburg.

Jack Milnes, who we met earlier in a series of letters from the mid-1780s, tells us a great deal about his business interests. He says that the family controlled over 50 per cent of the white cloth trade of the West Riding; furthermore, it is clear that Jack was buying fleeces from Saddleworth, Yorkshire, and importing fleece from Saxony. Indeed, Jack seems to have been a frequent traveller to the Continent, especially to what is Germany today. In the eighteenth century merino sheep were exported from Spain to Saxony; from then on Saxony became renowned for raw wool. By 1802 German wool was considered to be the finest in the world. It must have been on one of these business trips that Jack came across the Gotthardt family. The head of the family was Christian Frederick Gotthardt of Merseburg, Saxony (1738–1804), and is buried in the grounds of Westgate Chapel.

For a native of Saxony to be buried in Wakefield implies that Christian and his family came to Wakefield as economic migrants, on the back of the Milnes' family trading activities in Saxony. Therefore, it seems likely that Jack was making superfine cloth and that it was produced on the looms of the Shuttleworth family, who were co-religionists. William Burrell no doubt dyed the cloth and the Scott family finished the cloth. The whole process of cloth production would therefore have been undertaken by families from Westgate Chapel.

J&J NAYLOR

Since the early eighteenth century the Naylor family ran a large cloth-finishing business. By 1760, William and his brother Jeremiah, grandsons of the company founder, Ebenezer Naylor, are recorded as supplying cloth to Mr Fludyer, the leading London cloth merchant of the middle years of the eighteenth century, along with Daniel and Frank Maude. The Maudes had attended Westgate Chapel from the 1720s to 1750s. Indeed, Daniel Maude,

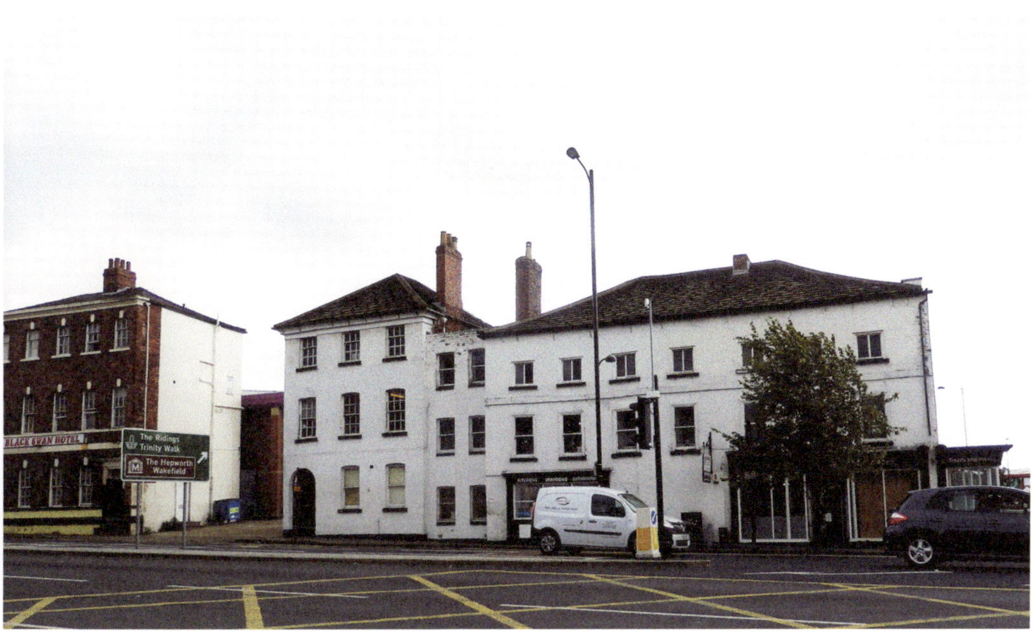

The Westgate home of Ebenezer Naylor, a leading cloth merchant who supplied the British army with cloth in the 1740s to 1790s.

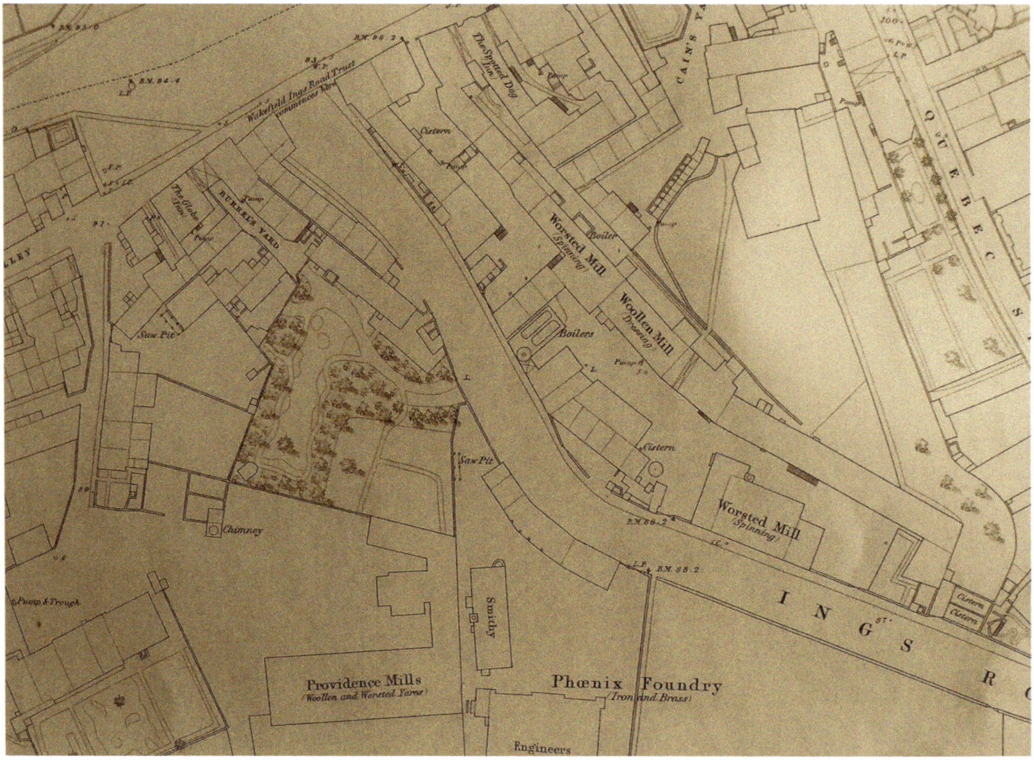

Map of the vast complex of workshops and buildings that made up J&J Naylor, the largest textile concern in Wakefield by 1805.

who built Alverthorpe Hall, was baptised at Westgate Chapel. The London trade was second only in importance to the export market, and so lucrative was a contract to provide dyed broadcloth to the army for production of soldier's coats that Jeremiah Naylor is reported as employing twenty-six or twenty-seven cloth dressers specifically to prepare the broadcloth to fulfil these orders.

Fludyer was an important man – one of the greatest cloth merchants of the eighteenth century. Samuel Fludyer (1704–68) was a dissenter, just like the Milnes and Naylors. He joined his father's business, which he greatly developed, and became one of the foremost cloth merchants. From 1738 till until his death he appears in the London directories in partnership with his brother Thomas as a warehouseman of Basinghall Street. In a list of merchant MPs compiled around 1754, in the Lowther mss, he is described as a 'great dealer in North and West country cloths'. Becoming a member of the Clothworkers' Company, he was elected to Common Council in 1734, became an alderman in 1751, was sheriff in 1754–55 and lord mayor in 1761–62. In 1753 he also became a director of the Bank of England, serving four terms, and was its deputy governor from 1766 until his death in 1768. In September 1755, in his capacity as sheriff, he presented an address from the lord mayor, aldermen and common council to George II expressing satisfaction at the King's safe return from his German dominions, and the king marked the occasion by knighting him. Four years later, on 14 November 1759, he was raised to the dignity of a baronetcy. The elaborate wig that he wore on becoming lord mayor in 1761 was depicted in William Hogarth's 1761 engraving *Five*

Orders of Periwigs. Through religion the Naylors were linked to one of the most important cloth merchanting housings in the country, and obtained lucrative government contracts.

William Naylor died on 29 March 1762 aged fifty-four, and was interred in the Westgate End Burial Ground. Mary Naylor, his wife, died on 24 October 1782 aged seventy-two. She was buried alongside her husband. Jeremiah Naylor died on 26 December 1764 aged forty-six; he was buried at Westgate End. The firm was continued by Jeremiah's sons, John and Jeremiah. By the 1770s, the firm was now known as John and Jeremiah Naylor. Henry Clarkson recalls:

> Mr John Naylor, the head of the firm, was a fine, portly looking man, always very well dressed, and wearing hair powder; and his wife was a stately handsome woman. He lived at Belle Vue in a house belonging to the Pilkington's of Chevet, since pulled down for the establishment of the present cemetery; and he used to come in, every morning, on horseback to the counting house which was at the bottom of Westgate, as were also the large warehouses. Mr Jeremiah Naylor, who was the working bee of the concern, and by no means such a polished gentleman as his brother, lived in the house on Westgate above Ings Road; and on Tuesday and Saturday mornings, he regularly drove to Leeds Market, to buy white and colour cloth in its unfinished state- each day being followed by a large waggon load or two of the cloth so bought, partly to be finished at their own works, and partly by cloth dressers in the town.
>
> My father and Mr Joseph Scott -grandfather of Miss Harriett Scott- were the principal cloth dressers and finishers for the Naylor's; the cloth being purchased by the firm then being in its raw state, where it underwent the process of 'cropping' and 'finishing' before its return to Naylor's' warehouse for packing and exportation. The white cloth had been previously dyed at the dye works, then carried on by Mr Joseph Holdsworth, at Belle Isle. Mr Scott lived, and had his works in the yard on the north side of Westgate known as 'Scott's Yard' and my father's works were the row of buildings on Westgate Bridge, now occupied as small shops. Each cloth dresser employed a number of men, called 'croppers' whose work was to cut off the rough surface of the cloth with large shears previously to it being pressed and finished. This old process once so important, has of course, been superseded by the use of machinery…to show the extent of the Naylor's business, I have heard my father say, that they purchased 1:13 of all the cloth manufactured in the West Riding.

With the end of the Seven Years' War and American Revolutionary Wars, coupled with the death of Fludyer, the firm shifted from government contracts to the army, to exporting to the new American states. In doing so they made huge profits. By 1805, the firm was trading broad and narrow cloth, fancy cloth, worsted, haberdashery and other goods with eleven firms in New York and Philadelphia – it was the second largest trading concern in Yorkshire with these American states. They were eclipsed only by Cookson's of Leeds. Henry Clarkson implies that the Naylors felt that they never eclipsed the Milnes or Heywoods; yet, when we look at the company's trading account we find that they had indeed eclipsed the Milnes'. We note Milnes, Heywood & Co., who only had three trading contracts with American states. Clearly, the Naylors, contrary to Henry Clarkson, were the leading cloth merchanting house of Wakefield and ranked second in the entire West Riding.

In 1806, in giving evidence to the government, Jeremiah Naylor noted that the company traded mostly with London or Portugal and had no interest to mechanise and change from the old method of hand finishing the cloth. Yet by 1820 the firm had started to mechanise as they insured a steam-powered mill in 1821 for the finishing of cloth and had begun to produce their own worsteds. The firm had clearly started to evolve, just like the Milnes had done forty years earlier, into merchant manufacturers.

This buoyant heyday for the family would not last. With the collapse of Wentworth's bank following the stock market crash of April 1825, the firm lost over £60,000 – millions in modern money – through the fraud of the bank's directors. The firm limped on until May 1829, but with liabilities of £149,000 and assets of £152,000 the firm collapsed. Unsold goods in Lima were valued at £20,000, Rio some £30,000 of stock and at Buenos Aires another £12,000. Earl Fitzwilliam offered the Naylors a bridging loan to save the company, but the company accounts were to tangled with those of Wentworth's bank that it proved impossible to save the company. The debt on the books from unpaid bills was a staggering £125,000, and a further £9,500. With their failure, J&J Naylor owed the Holdsworths a staggering £12,765 19*s* 4*d* – a veritable fortune at the time, and worth many millions in 2019. Needless to say, William Holdsworth passed the mill on Westgate back to Rachel Milnes, owing £875.

The premises of J&J Naylor were sold in 1830. Joseph Barker took over the premises before rebuilding Thornes Mill in 1838, and from 1858 it was tenanted and then owned by Mathew Porritt Stonehouse.

John Naylor died on 24 January 1830, aged seventy-nine, and was buried at All Saints' Parish Church. He was a member of Westgate Chapel all his life and had been appointed a trustee in 1774, a post he held until he died. William Naylor died on 26 March 1839 aged sixty-four and was also buried in All Saints' Parish Church. He died on a journey from Manchester to

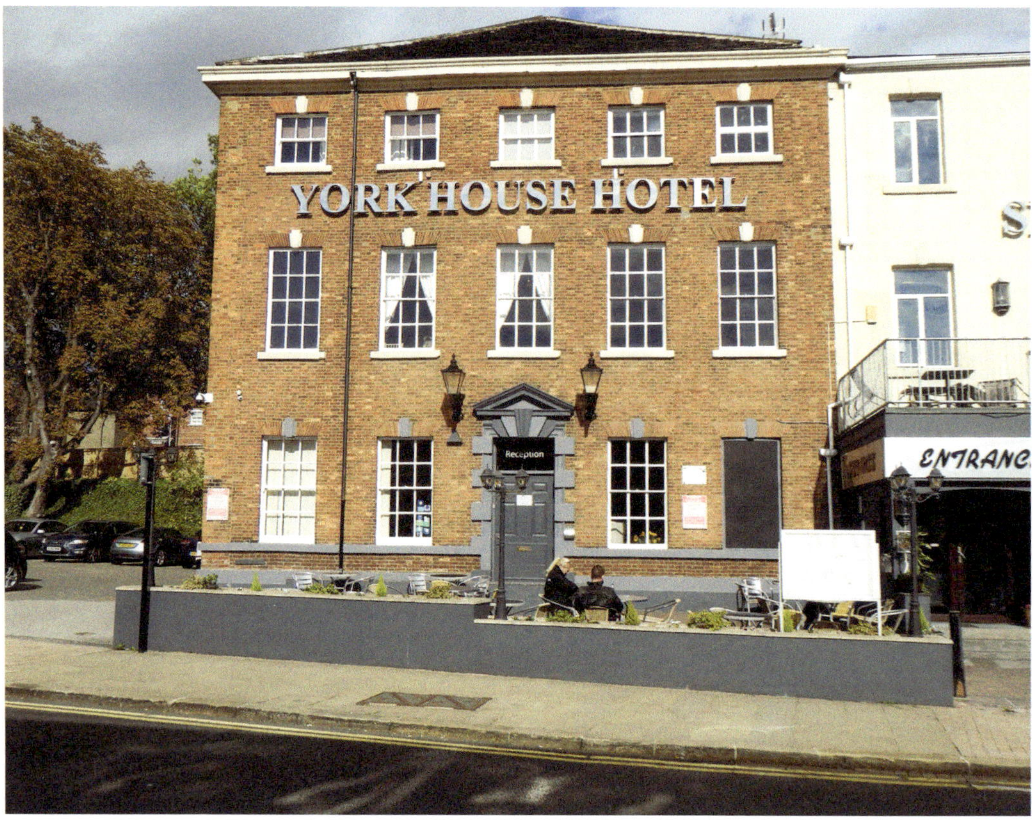

York House, home of William Naylor.

Wakefield; his body was found in the coach upon arriving in Wakefield. He had left the family firm before its collapse and lived in York House on Drury Lane. Jeremiah Naylor was very much a Tory and was a member of the Pitt Club, yet was also a chapel member for a time – or at least paid pew rent.

The former J&J Naylor premises remained in the textile trade. Joseph Barker took over the premises before building Thornes Mill in 1838, and from 1858 it was tenanted and then owned by Mathew Porritt Stonehouse. The collapse of J&J Naylor precipitated the collapse of the Holdsworths' major businesses as dyers and cloth manufacturers and sent shock wave through the woollen district around Wakefield, from which it never recovered.

With J&J Naylor collapsing, the smaller manufacturers that supplied them with goods had to find other markets, which they did. Naylor's supply chain was extensive and encompassed most of the West Riding. It is reckoned one-thirteenth of the cloth of the Riding passed through the firm in 1805 – a huge amount, but a fraction of the cloth that had been handled by Jack Milnes twenty-five years earlier.

Yet even so, when we look at the mills that Wakefield did have, we don't see the picture of terminal decline until the twentieth century. Compared to Bradford, Halifax or Leeds the woollen trade did not undergo large-scale expansion, but coal mining and the corn trade flourished. Wakefield's wealth had been built on the woollen trade since the sixteenth century. The nineteenth century was a time of flux, when the old domestic system of wool cloth production was shifting to the factory system. At the same the Napoleonic Wars, particularly the Napoleonic blockade, resulted in economic stagnation and collapse of the woollen trade. The years 1806–16 caused a number of mills in Wakefield to fail, namely those of Daniel Washington, Jonathan Chambers, Robert Bakewell and the Wards at Flanshaw. Jack Milnes, Thomas Lumb and 'Bob' Bakewell were all leaders of the anti-war movement. Economic stress drove mechanisation in the 1770s and 1780s. The years 1790–1803 continued economic stress on the domestic system, and witnessed the centralisation of skills into 'proto' factories. The peace of Amiens resulted in a boom for the cloth trade, witnessing steam-powered mills being built across the town; yet, within a few years these businesses had 'all gone to the wall' as they could not compete with the larger manufacturers. In this Leeds led the way, with Benjamin Gott at the forefront of factory development. Therefore, we have several factors in play: politics of Whig vs Tory, the Church vs religious radicals (we must remember Unitarian belief was made illegal in 1698 and only tolerated under law in 1813), economic stagnation occasioned by the Napoleonic Wars, and banking failure leading to the collapse of a major West Riding merchanting business, the second largest in the West Riding in 1805.

The Milnes family were just one of several Unitarian families that invested heavily in textile production and mechanisation. The Lumbs, Holdsworths and Marriotts all played an important part in the wool trade. Failure to expand commercially in textile production was related, as we said earlier, to the price of land in Wakefield along the banks of the River Chald on the Ings. It is surely no coincidence that this land, some of the most valuable in Wakefield due to its close proximity to the cattle market for pasture for cattle to graze upon, was never developed for mills and heavy industry until the late nineteenth century. And that the development of mills at Silcoates, Alverthorpe and Flanshaw was in part due to the price of land here being lower. Another major factor was access to running water and coal from the Haigh Moor Collieries to power the steam engines. The trade in fleece declined dramatically after 1842, with the number of wool merchants declining by 50 per cent in ten years. This thesis has shown that Unitarians financed the mechanisation of the woollen trade in Wakefield, which for a time was a boom industry until banking failure in 1825 ended the surge.

DYEING FOR WAKEFIELD

In the eighteenth century cloth could be dyed in two ways: by the piece (i.e. woven pieces of cloth) or by the thread (i.e. the yarn was dyed and then spun prior to weaving). This meant that a clothier could readily supply large lengths of cloth of different colours. Cloth woven with dyed thread had a longer production time. This method of production produced a much stronger and more consistent shade through the cloth. It was far costlier than cloth dyed in the piece, as the clothier had to buy the cloth ready dyed in far longer lengths than the cloth dyed once woven. It was – and is – easier to buy 1,000 m of cloth with 10 m dyed blue and the rest another colour, than having to buy 1,000 m of cloth and only needing 10 m initially in the chosen colour. Dyeing the yarn before weaving gave a better quality of colour, but it meant that a mill had to produce minimum quantities of cloths of different colours, whereas the mills producing cloth that was dyed later could produce a cheaper product as the looms produced a natural cloth, using yarn that was not as well sorted or selected as the higher-grade fabric.

BURRELLS DYE WORKS

In the 1760s, the principle dyers in Wakefield were, according to an eighteenth-century diarist, Robert Lumb and William Burrell. We discussed the Lumbs previously. William Burrell Sr (1712–71) married co-religionist Ruth Scott (1717–80). He was the founder of the family's dye works. The works were on Thornes Lane, on land rented from the lord of the manor. On 11 February 1774, William Burrell Jr (1745–76) and his wife Priscilla were the occupiers of the land and dye works. After William's death Priscilla married Jonathan Chambers (we met both of them earlier concerning Thornes Lane Mill), who was named as running the company in a deed of 14 May 1779 for the benefit of Richard Burrell (1751–1835) and Joseph Burrell (1743–1812), who married firstly Martha Beckett (1740–87) and secondly Hannah Holdsworth (1744–1826). William Burrell (1772–1842), son of William and Priscilla, was baptised at Westgate on 28 June 1772, his father having died before he was born.

In 1793, William Burrell Jr, at the age of twenty-one, took over the management of the family business from his stepfather Jonathan Chambers, who we met earlier. A year later, in 1794, William gave £10 10s to form the Royal Wakefield Volunteers, and in 1798 a further £10

10s to the same cause. He paid game tax in 1796 and is described as 'William Burrell Junior, Gentleman of Thornes'.

He married Frances Morville on 21 September 1797. He was a trustee of Westgate Chapel, like his father before him. On 8 July 1796 he took out an £800 mortgage from Jane Rooke to buy the copyhold of the land where the dye works was built. By 8 May 1812 William had paid of £740 of the outstanding balance. On 31 May 1805 he sold over 5 acres of land in Thornes, as well as five houses, a cottage and a barn to raise capital to pay his debts as well as to gain money to buy cloth, which he then finished for the export market. He appears to have taken out vast loans to buy stock, notably cloth, which he dyed and finished and then sold on for profit. The profit was evidently sufficient as he was able to cancel out the debt and to leave him with cash in hand. In order to raise capital, on 5 September 1812 he took out a mortgage for £1,000 from co-religionist and chapel trustee Richard Rodes Milnes, acting for Milnes, Leatham & Co. However, the ongoing economic downturn meant that he was struggling to pay off this mortgage, and to try and rectify this, on 5 May 1817, William took out another a mortgage, this time for some £1,200 from Wentworth, Chaloner & Rishworth to pay off the £530 owed to Milnes & Co. and to buy stock for export. This gamble clearly failed, given the economic conditions of the time, as on 14 September 1818 yet another mortgage was taken out on the dye works and mill. This time it was for the sum of £3,500, again from Wentworth, Chaloner & Rishworth, to pay off accumulated debts of £3,160. The gamble seems to have paid off for a time as Burrell had no need to raise capital for nearly four years. On 21 June 1822 Benjamin Gott, the great Leeds Industrialist, advanced a loan of £2,617 to pay off debts, which he had managed to bring down to £1,933 due to the improving economic climate. Despite this hefty loan to stave off bankruptcy, on 4 May 1824 William Burrell was declared bankrupt. The case was brought by Robert Smithson, Thomas Charnock and Thomas Livesey of Haigh Moor Colliery for unpaid bills on coal deliveries. In consequence, his estate was advertised for auction in the *Leeds Intelligencer* of Thursday 26 August 1824, on page 1. His estate was broken down into various lots:

Lot 1: A large warehouse and shop at the top of Queen Street, fronting onto the corn market, latterly occupied by Mr Otty, grocer.
Lot 2: A three-floor warehouse standing in Kirkgate, reported as converted into a good dwelling house.
Lot 3: Two houses, with stable, outbuildings and garden adjoining the warehouse in Kirkgate, occupied by John Melton and Thomas Backhouse.
Lot 4: A pew in Wakefield parish church of eight sittings. On the north side of the middle isle, near the pulpit.
Lot 5: Two freehold cottages with gardens and waste ground at Brandy Carr containing two roods of land (1 rood = ¼ acre, therefore ½ ace). In addition, a further 7 ½ acres at Brandy Carr.
Lot 6: House containing four rooms and a kitchen on the ground floor, four lodging rooms and closets on the second floor, and four lodging rooms in the attics. Also stables, outbuildings, gardens, plantation with land adjoining, 4,647 square yards in Thornes adjoining the River Calder. In addition, a croft with dyeing house and warehouse – some 8,000 square yards. An additional plot of land in Commercial Street – some 303 square yards.

The sale of his estate was managed by Messrs Foljambie and Dixon, solicitors of Wakefield. The auction was held at 6 p.m. on Friday 10 September 1824 at the White Hart Inn, Wakefield. According to Pigot's 1828 trade directory, Thomas Bell had taken possession of the Thornes Lane dye works.

In his bankruptcy proceedings, William is listed as having latterly 'exercised and carryed on the business of a merchant and dyer, by buying quantities of woollen goods and other merchandise and dyeing and finishing the same and afterwards exporting the same from England to Russia and other places beyond the seas'. William died a broken man in 1842 and is buried with his wife and children in the burial ground of Westgate Chapel.

MILNES DYE WORKS

The Milnes family controlled the sale of large quantities of undyed white wool broadcloth. Keen to provide more than white cloth, Robert Milnes had constructed a dye works shortly before his death in 1734 at Belle Vue, on the river frontage. The works were managed by the Lumb family – again, Westgate Chapel men. The diarist Brearley adds that Mr Lumb was the dyer to the Milnes family and kept fifteen or sixteen men in the summer and nine or ten in the winter.

The dye works were conveyed to Richard Lumb in 1775, and thence John Lumb and Joseph Holdsworth as partners. The partnership was dissolved on 1 January 1781 and the business was carried on by Joseph Holdsworth, who bought the works in 1789.

Rather than purchase expensive indigo dye, the Holdsworths produced their own dye and, to do so, purchased hundreds of acres of land in Lincolnshire to grow woad – the business was conducted by the Yorkshire Woad Company, owned by the Holdsworths. Upon Joseph Holdsworth Sr's death in July 1826 he was succeeded by his son Joseph (1789–1857). Joseph Jr enlarged the works at Belle Vue. He had married Eliza Holy from Sheffield in 1822. She joined the Wesleyan congregation at West Parade where her funeral sermon was preached in 1846. With the failure of the banking firm of Wentworth Chaloner and Rishworth, in which Joseph had placed his reserve capitol, it placed the company in financial difficulties. With his death in 1857, Joseph's sons, Joseph Hulme Holdsworth and Thomas Holy Holdsworth, succeeded to the business.

The business was given up on 17 July 1868. The site of the works was purchased by the Yorkshire Electric Tramways Syndicate Inc in 1904 and become a tram depot; it is now a bus depot.

BANKING

The burgeoning trade in wool and, from the late eighteenth century, cattle resulted in the need for available funds in the form of hard cash by the merchants dealing with these products. For the cloth trade to function the merchant needed cash payments to buy cloth and pay his journeymen's wages. Therefore, the need to transmute bills of exchange (for example from payments for cloth shipments) into regular supplies of cash resulted in the formation of banks in the town from the 1780s. The use of bills of exchange made every businessman a banker of sorts, and the pressing need for circulating currency was an inducement for some merchants to enter into banking.

In Wakefield that was James Milnes Sr, a prominent member of Westgate Chapel. He was providing mortgages from the 1770s. The economic slump and major recession of 1772 and 1775, and that of 1778–83, which witnessed a collapse in the export market of broadcloth and worsteds, no doubted prompted James into providing loans as a more secure means of revenue.

He was a wealthy merchant and used his fortune to buy land. Indeed, his landholdings came to around 1,000 acres, including 82 acres at Morley, 11 acres at Hunslet, 100 acres at Darfield, 35 acres at Ardsley, and 95 acres at Gildersome including a corn mill. He invested £2,000 in the Aire and Calder Navigation Company at 4 per cent in 1774, and at his death in 1791 had stock worth £13,000 in the company. He invested a further £1,000 in other canal shares. Turnpike securities came to £2,300, including £1,000 in the Sheffield and Wakefield Turnpike. He bought the mortgage for Jacksons Bridge Mill at Jacksons Bridge, Huddersfield, on 15 January 1790 from William Shackleton of Wakefield and Henry Lee of Eastmoor. The mill comprised 'the house, corn mill and drying kiln with a small close of land called Holt Holm adjoining the mill'. He purchased land at Oulton in 1748 situated at Fleet, and in 1763 bought four-sixths of the royalty of Oulton from Toby Birkes for £1,200, which included 37 acres of valuable agricultural land. In 1765 he bought three closes near Newmarket and 10 acres at Patrick Green for £300.

As well as buying land, mortgages were big business with huge profits to be made. In 1770 he provided a whopping mortgage of £10,500 to George Smirthwaite, a London wool-stapler, to develop Newmarket Colliery, with the nearby canal being used to take the coals to market. In October 1789 James Milnes provided £2,000 5s to Joshua Raynor of Manchester, housebuilder, to build a series of speculative properties in that place. The mortgage was agreed at 5 per cent interest. Milnes owned extensive land in East Yorkshire, notably at Wallingfen, near Howden.

James Milnes died in 1791 and he was succeeded by his spendthrift son James Milnes. James Jr became an MP and a leading figure of London society. His father had built Thornes House for him. James Jr continued his father's banking activity and loaned money to Ebenezer Aldred, who we mentioned earlier. He left the management of the business to William Dawson, John Craven and Joseph Burrell – all Westgate Chapel men. Interest on loans, as well as on rents from land, brought in huge wealth; between 12 May 1793 and 12 May 1796 his income from interest on loans was a whopping £3,182 3s 9*d*. In the same period rents from Wallingfen land brought in £3,142 14s. James Milnes died in 1805 and lies with his wife, father and mother in the catacombs beneath Westgate Chapel. He passed his wealth and land to his nephews, Benjamin and Daniel Gaskell. Joseph Burrell died in 1812 and is buried beneath Westgate Chapel. William Dawson and John Craven managed the estates and banking firm on behalf of the Gaskells until 1824 when Dawson emigrated to America and became the first governor of Baltimore.

However, it is telling that after the death in 1791 of James Milnes Sr that Wakefield gained its first banking firm proper. From 1792 the banking firm of Ingram, Kennett and Ingram played an important role in the commerce of Wakefield. The partners were Francis Ingram, Benjamin Kennett and Abraham Richard Ingram, the second son of Francis Ingram. By 1772 Francis Ingram was heavily involved in slave trading and financed 122 slaving trips, which were responsible for enslaving 41,412 people. His bank was funded on the trafficking of human lives. The bank experienced fiscal difficulties in 1808 when it was discovered that the Halifax co-partnership was in debt to the Wakefield co-partnership. Bank House, on Westgate, was the company's headquarters.

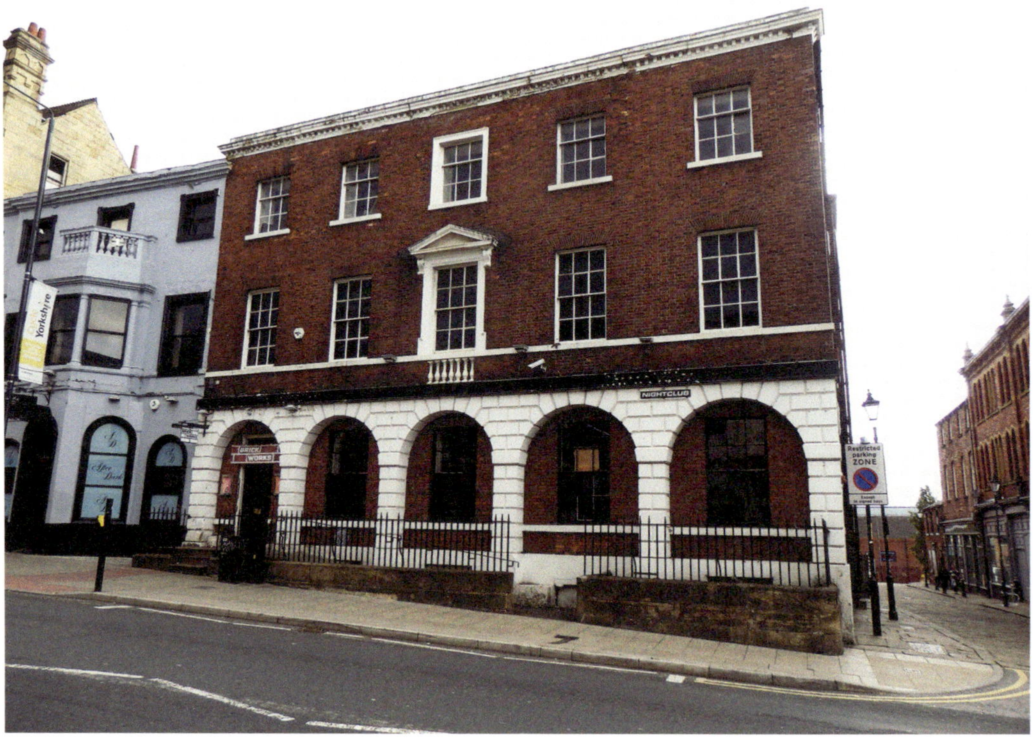

The banking premises and home of Francis Ingram, banker and slave master.

A second bank appeared in Wakefield not long after Ingram had gone bust. Richard Rodes Milnes, the second son of Richard Slate Milnes and trustee of Westgate Chapel, founded with John Leatham and Thomas Tew, Milnes, Leatham & Co. in 1808. John Leatham had provided quasi-banking services for customers at his shop in the Market Place at Pontefract for some time before entering into a formal partnership with James Jackson, Thomas Tew and Edward Trueman in 1801. Initially, service was available in Pontefract and Doncaster, but a third branch was opened in Wakefield when the business of Ingram, Kennet and Ingram was purchased in 1808 by Rodes Milnes, who immediately went into partnership with Leatham and Tew as Milnes Leatham & Co. With the death of Richard Rodes Milnes in 1834 the firm adopted the title Leatham, Tew & Co. and remained so until the amalgamation with Barclay & Co. Ltd in 1906.

A third bank had appeared, styled Townend & Rishworth, commencing trading in 1802 and drew on the London bank of Boldero. Appearing in various iterations, the bank was formed *c.* 1765 when the partnership of Boldero, Carter and Boldero split. One of the successor firms became Boldero, Kendall & Adey, then Boldero, Lushington, Boldero and variants. The bank failed on 13 June 1814 and collapsed Townend and Rishworth.

With the failure of Townend and Rishworth, the York firm of Wentworth & Chaloner moved into Wakefield, opening a branch styled Wentworth, Chaloner & Rishworth. Like two previous banks, the firm had a very unhappy history. The London stock market collapsed in April 1825

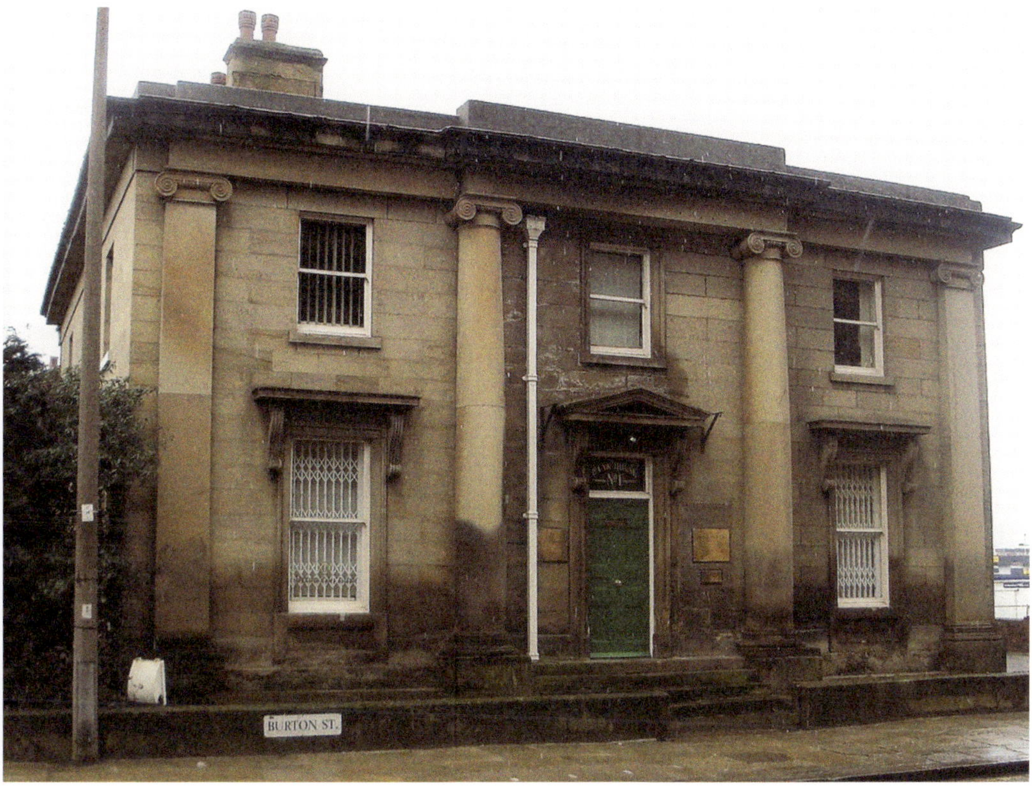

Bank House, on Burton Street, home of the Wakefield Savings Bank, which was managed for a time by Richard Rodes Milnes, son of Richard Slater Milnes MP. The bank was financed by his uncle John Pemberton Heywood, who, like Rodes Milnes, was trustee of Westgate Chapel.

and in December that year the bank failed and was asset stripped. None of the Wakefield creditors were ever paid. In consequence, the Huddersfield Banking Company opened an agency in Wakefield. In 1832 the Wakefield Banking Company was formed, becoming in 1840 the Wakefield & Barnsley Union Bank with the purchase of Beckett & Co. of Barnsley. The bank later merged with Barclays. Another ill-fated Wakefield bank was the Wakefield Building Society. In the 1970s the shock discovery was made that the present and previous general managers had, over many years, embezzled a fortune. The society merged immediately with the Halifax Building Society.

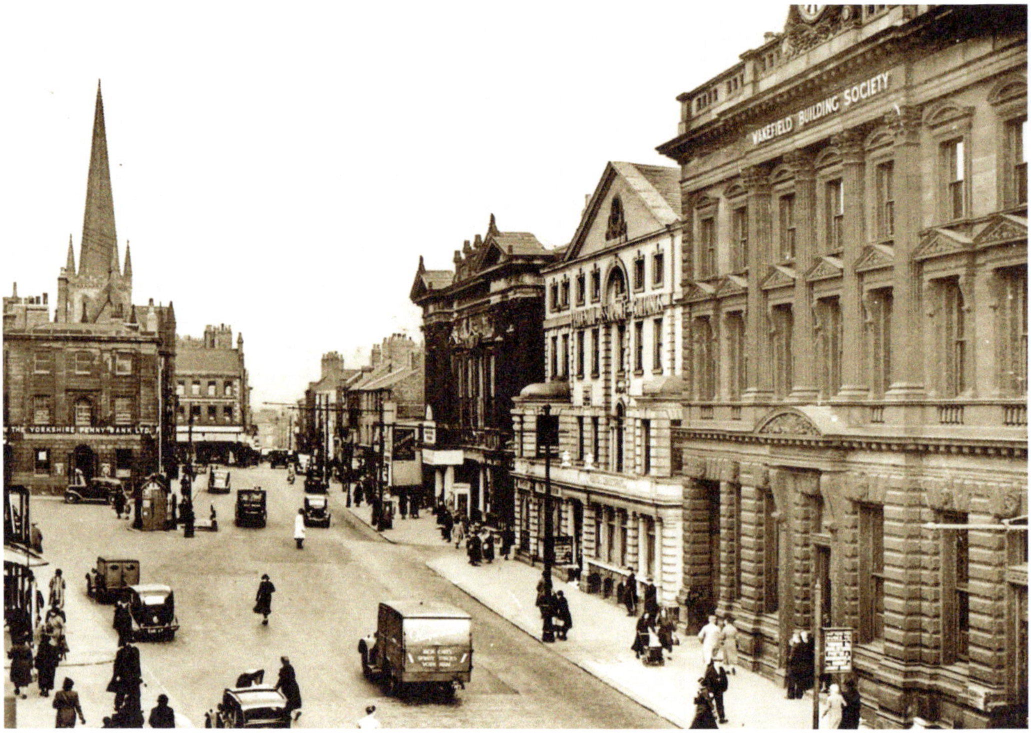

On the right of the image we see the 'Three Graces' of Westgate: the Corn Exchange, the Great Black Bull Hotel and the banking premises of the Wakefield and Barnsley Union Bank, which is today a nightclub.

COAL MINING

Coal had been extracted in Wakefield since the Middle Ages, but it was not until the eighteenth century that mining developed into a major industry. The first concern we have details of is Newmarket Colliery, which was in operation by 1775. The concern was bankrolled by Unitarian James Milnes. The coal was transported to the coal staithes on the newly opened canal for export. When this pit closed in 1983 it was one of the oldest working pits in the UK. It was sunk in 1837 by the coal kings of the time – the Fentons. It was later owned by the Charlesworths. Newmarket workings ran as far as Lane Ends under Stanley and are said to be the cause of subsidence at Stanley Church. At one time 99 per cent of men who lived at Bottomboat worked at this colliery.

BY 1790 Josiah Smithson had developed the Haigh Moor Colliery along the Alverthorpe Valley. William Fenton was extracting coals from Outwood, which developed into Lofthouse Pit. At Flockton the Milnes family developed a colliery system, with one of their pits being Cap House Colliery. Beginning in the 1780s they laid out a wooden 'Newcastle Road' – i.e. an early railway, perhaps the first in the West Riding, to carry the coals from Flockton to the canal. The railway witnessed the building of the world's first railway tunnel and railway viaduct, but only the latter remains. James Milnes of Flockton (not to be confused with either James Milnes of Wakefield) was the consulting engineers to Smithson at Haigh Moor. The railway was relaid with iron rails in 1825 to provide the necessary transport for coal from the colliery. The New Flockton Colliery finally closed in 1893 after a prolonged strike. During the nineteenth century more mines were sunk so that there were forty-six small mines in Wakefield and the surrounding area by 1869. The National Coal Board eventually became Wakefield's largest employer, with Manor Colliery on Cross Lane and Park Hill colliery at Eastmoor surviving until 1982. Nationally important innovation's in colliery management took place in 1863 at Methley, Streethouse, Snydale and Whiwood collieries – part of the Briggs empire of collieries, ironworks, brick and glass works. Henry Briggs and his son decided to promote a scheme of co-operative management, under which both customers, officials and workmen could share in the profitability of the undertaking. The scheme provided for the division of the profits after proper provision for depreciation, etc. And, after setting aside a sum to remunerate the invested capital, it was to be shared equally between shareholders and employees as a bonus percentage on the money invested in shares, or for non-shareholders as a similar percentage on wages earned during the year.

There were no obligation for workmen or officials to put their share of the bonus back to buy shares, but many did so, and therefore they received not only the current bonus on earnings, but also the dividend on shares bought out of past bonuses; in addition, it was provided that the employees should elect two members to the board of directors, provided that no strikes took place and that all disputes in the event of dissatisfaction should be settled by arbitration. This scheme proved highly satisfactory for many years and upward of £40,000 in bonus pay was divided among the work people, and more than 300 became shareholders.

To enable this to be arranged a new company was registered as a limited liability company with a capital of £450,000, of which £247,000 was to be paid up and issued in the form of shares to shareholders. Included with the colliery assets and farms taken over by the new company, the Yorkshire Coal and Steam Ship Company also became part, which had invested £60,000 in four ships called the *Altona* and *Marianne Briggs* of 700 tons each and the *Dinnington* and *Whitwood* of 500 tons and 400 tons respectively. The first two traded from Goole to Hamburg and the other two from Goole to Rouen. The large boats on the Hamburg run had reasonable passenger accommodation for fifteen persons each.

From 1865 to 1868 the chairman of the company was Mr Henry Briggs, followed by Henry Currer Briggs from 1868 to 1881, then Arthur Currer Briggs. The company was nationalised in 1947/48.

Henry Briggs was a confirmed Liberal and believed in deciding his own code of conduct; he was one not easily deterred from his objectives. He was a most conscientious Unitarian and spent much of his spare time in promoting the education of the young. He was noted as a keen and regular Sunday school teacher at Westgate Chapel, Wakefield, and on many occasions acted as a lay preacher and occupied the pulpit when the need arose. He was a powerful man and eminently just, and, being 6 feet 2½ inches in height, made a notable figure. His wife ably supported him and, as she was 6 feet in height, they were noted as an imposing couple.

Other important pits around Wakefield included Manor Colliery and Park Hill Colliery. Originally owned by the Hudson family, Park Hill was worked from 1863 up to 1983. In 1919 a fire destroyed most of the surface buildings, trapping men down the pit. The ventilation fan was stopped to prevent fumes being carried into the workings while a rescue team was assembled. Many men were put out of work by the fire, not returning to work until the damage was repaired. Tragedy struck again in 1974 when nine miners became trapped by a 200-ton roof falling more than 600 feet down. A rescue operation was mounted after 12 yards of roof caved in around 250 yards behind the men. After clawing their way through boulders and rubble the trapped men managed to get through an 18-inch gap, where they met members of the three rescue teams that had been sent in to dig them out. A model village of more than 150 back-to-back houses was built at New Sharlston from 1864 to house Sharlston Colliery Company workers. The houses cost just over £100 each and the streets were named Long Row, Crossley Street and High Street. A Methodist chapel and a day school were built on Crossley Street. The homes became the property of the National Coal Board in 1947. In 1961 twenty-eight back-to-back houses were converted into fourteen through houses. The school and the chapel have been demolished. Many will also remember Roundwood and Manor collieries.

No pitheads survive in Wakefield. The proud mining history of the city is preserved at the National Coal Mining Museum for England at Cap House Colliery.

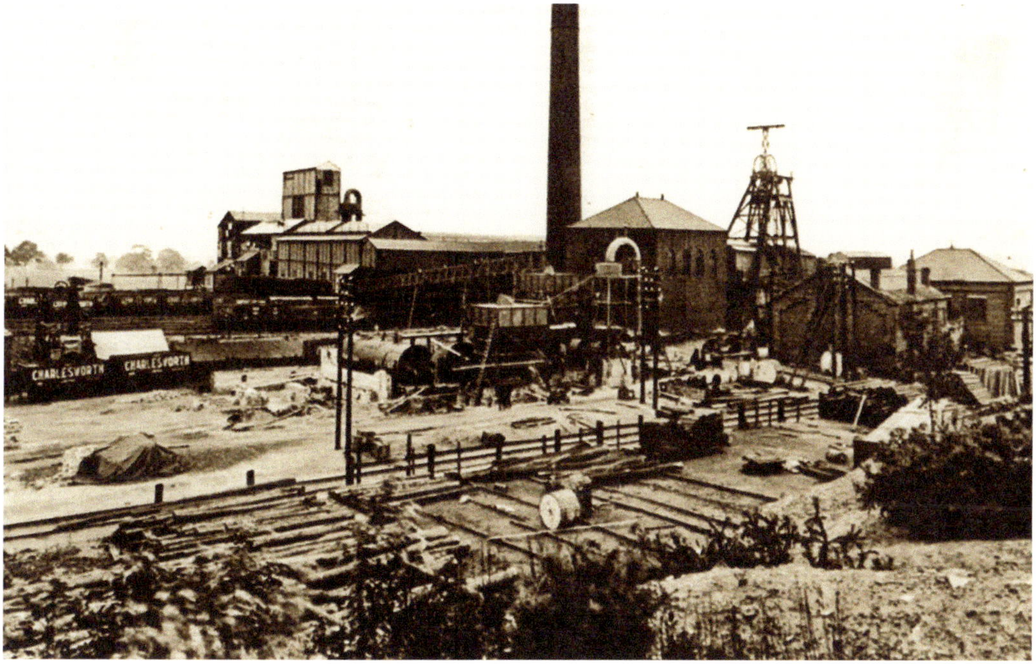

Newmarket Colliery, *c.* 1910. The colliery had been started in the 1770s by the Milnes family of Westgate Chapel.

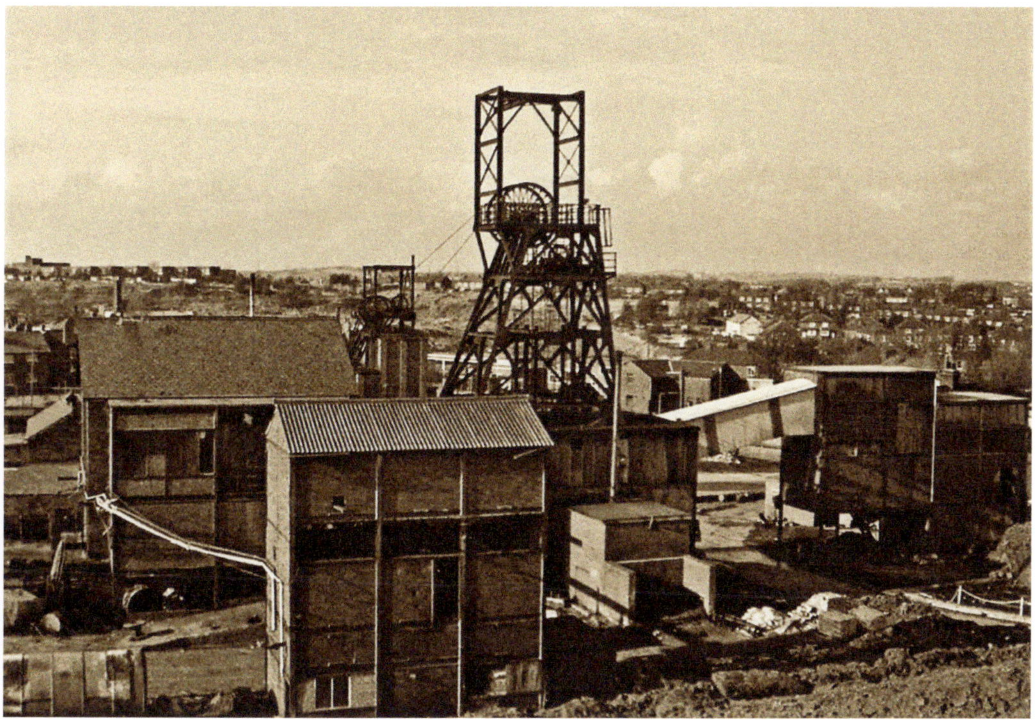

Manor Colliery off Dewsbury Road in Wakefield. The site now holds housing.

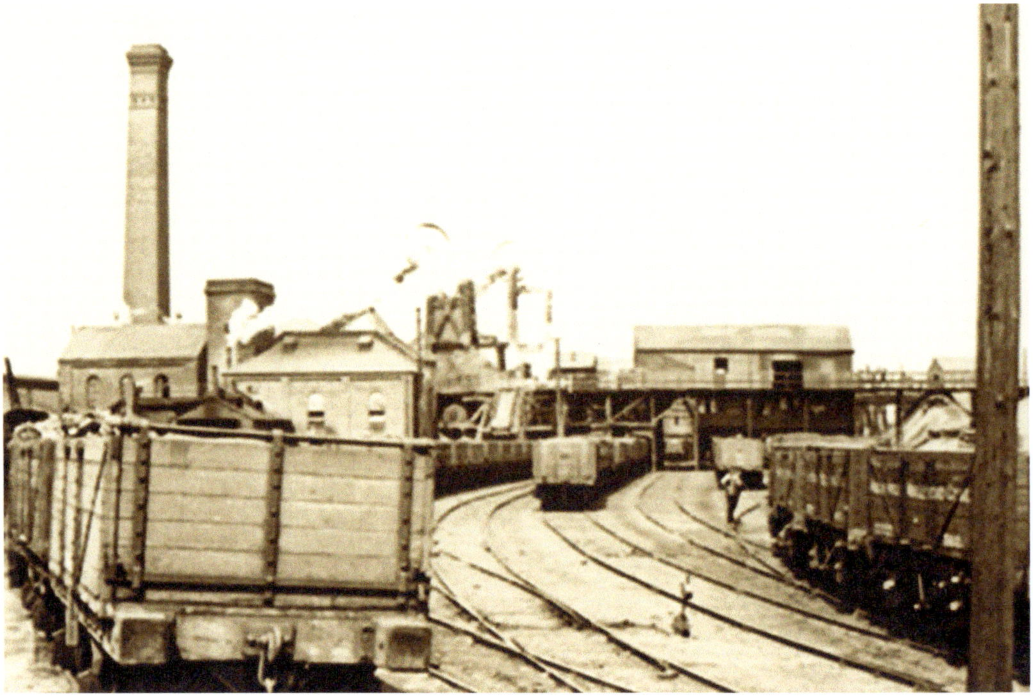

Above, below and next page: Four views of the now long-gone Park Hill Colliery on Eastmoor. It was worked from 1863 up to 1983. In recent years a pit wheel has been erected to commemorate the mine and its men.

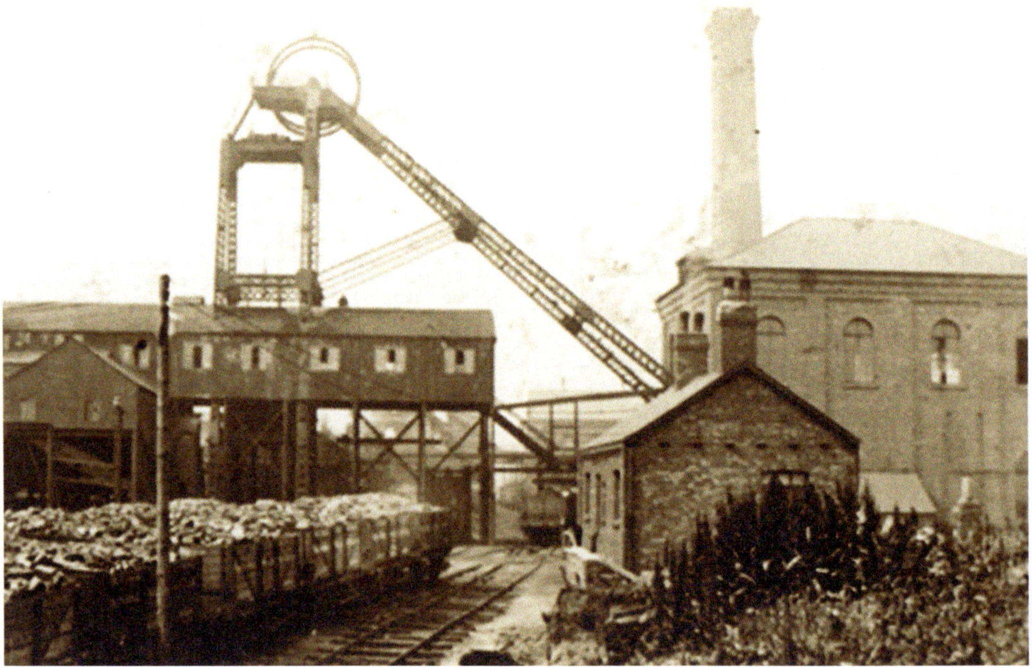

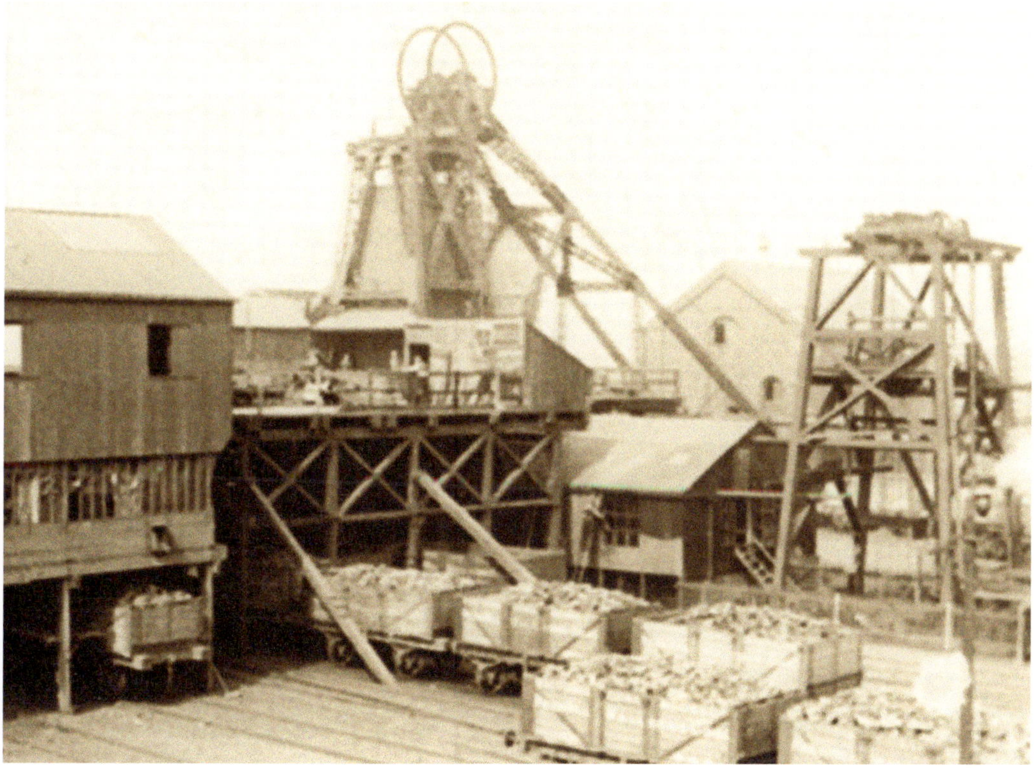

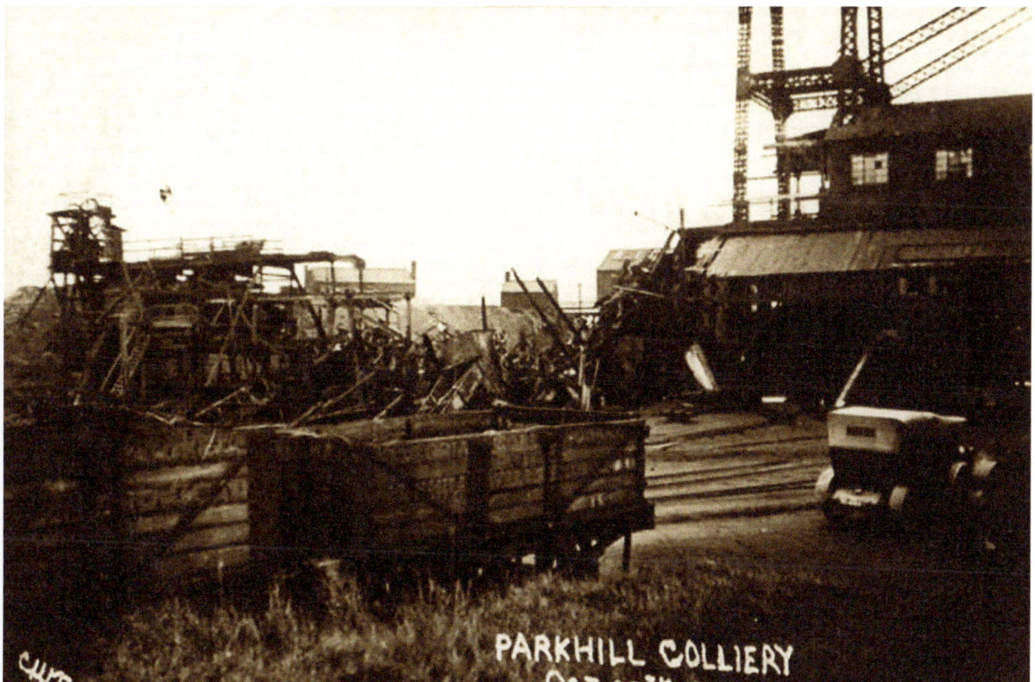
PARKHILL COLLIERY
OCT. 27TH 1919
CWN.

OTHER INDUSTRIES

A vital trade in any big city was construction. One of the largest concerns, with over 300 staff, was Drake & Warters Ltd. This was founded in 1922 by Charles Henry Drake and Robert Warters and was the largest privately owned builders and shop fitting company in the country in the 1940s and 1950s. The first headquarters of the company was a small wooden and corrugated-iron shed and a converted railway carriage in Back Lane, behind the Playhouse Cinema. The transport department consisted of a small handcart, and timber was carried from Westgate station to the works. It was around this cart that the team spirit for which the company was famed was created – everyone from directors to office boy buckled when it came to fetching timber. As the business prospered it became harder and harder to push the cart up Back Lane. Mr Drake brought one of his ideas into use, and his belt driven Scott motorcycle with side car, was used to tow the handcart instead. Eventually, however, the handcart gave up the struggle when the wheels collapsed. By 1927, the firm had developed sufficient capital to be able to purchase the cabinetmaking works of Hall & Armitage of Thornhill Street. The premises were rapidly expanded with the yard area in front of one of the buildings being in-filled with timber-built stores and workshops. In these early days most types of work were undertaken, be they large or small

By 1936 the upstairs downstairs existence was no longer viable, and the New Wells estate was purchased. In place of tennis courts, gardens and an orchard, a 50,000-square-foot factory was built. In this new factory, seventy-four of the most up-to-date machines in the country were installed.

The machines installed in the factory made it possible for rough planks to be brought in, put through various processes and machines and turned out as high-grade furniture or shop fittings. The fact that freshly hewn timber could be taken into the factory and turned out three weeks later in the shape of furniture was due to the use of a drying kiln, which was the only one in the north of England at the time. A total of 700 hundred cubic feet of timber could be stacked in the kiln, and the workers at the control board studied dials and graphs to keep correct temperatures.

Inside the main shop were saws that could cut through oak boards faster than a warm knife through butter. A double-ended tenon machine, one of the most modern in the world, could produce 2,000 tenons a day. A man working with hand tools could average around twenty a day. There is little in the line of woodworking that it could not do. Nearby was an electric router, which operated at anything from 18 to 24,000 revolutions a minute. In fact, the electrical supply to the factory had to be stepped up to give direct drive to this machine, which took five minutes to slow down when the brake was not used. With this machine it was possible to cut out a person's name, in wood, in almost the exact handwriting of the writer, except at a larger scale.

The new factory was completed by 1939 and also included the boardroom, which was described as the nearest thing that Wakefield had to a top flight Hollywood executive's office, seen in films of the period. During the 1930s, shopfitting was undertaken all across the British Isles. Charlie Drake once remarked that there was not a single town or city in England, Ireland, Scotland, Wales, the Isle of Man or the Channel Islands where there was not some product of Drake & Warters. You could go into London's Regent Street, Leicester Square or the Strand and find Drake & Warters shopfronts and interior fittings. The firm fitted out some of the biggest firms in Leeds and Bradford. Many multiples were catered for, including Timothy Whites & Tailors, Boots, Maypole & Meadow, Homes and Colonial, Lupton's, Schofield's and many more.

So far as shopfitting was concerned, the company were able to dismantle existing fittings, build a new shopfront (or the whole building for that matter) and equip the interior in the space of the shop closing on a Saturday evening and opening on the Monday at 9 a.m. ready for business! The building side was carried out by Harry Hainsworth Ltd, which became Drake & Warters (Builders) Ltd in 1935, with the sole owner and managing director being Charlie Drake. Drake & Warters (Builders) Ltd in the post-war years built many schools in the West Riding of Yorkshire, which Drake & Warters Ltd provided the internal fittings for.

During the Second World War the firm built seventy-two landing craft for D-Day, coastal defence fortifications from Bridlington to Whitby, and constructed army camps near Beverley. The firm also built 150,000 wooden prefab houses in the late 1940s.

The 1950s were a period of great optimism, with shop fitting continuing to be the main source of income, though the production of manufactured joinery declined. New railway engine sheds were constructed at Wakefield Westgate station and at the Belle Vue Motive Power Depot. New office blocks and banks were built and fitted out in Wakefield and across Yorkshire. Experiments were also made at producing flat-pack furniture at this time. Tenders were also submitted for providing the fittings for the new development at Primrose Hill, Wakefield. The firm also supplied new fittings for the shop Double Two and refitted the Empire Cinema. However, large companies like Boots were developing their own in-house shop-fitting companies. The firm ceased trading in the late 1970s, and the Anchor Housing complex occupies part of the site of the factory.

Beer and bread were staples of the Victorian diet. So much so that Wakefield grew increasingly important as a centre for trading corn for brewing and bread making. By 1843, the corn trade in Wakefield was noted as employing 'about three hundred vessels of from fifty to ninety tons each'. The corn market, held on Friday, was second only to that of London. Ranges of large corn warehouses still stand on the banks of the river.

Malt, which was formerly brought from other districts, was made at Wakefield to a very large extent. By 1890 the city had a proliferation of malthouses, with many built in the narrow yards running from the principle streets or were vast complexes built along the banks of the River Calder, where between Wakefield Bridge South to Belle Isle no fewer than sixteen malthouses (some with kilns) could be found. Here, too, were three corn mills. For the sale of corn, a Corn Exchange was built on Westgate in 1820. It was replaced by a far larger building that stood opposite at the top of Westgate in 1837.

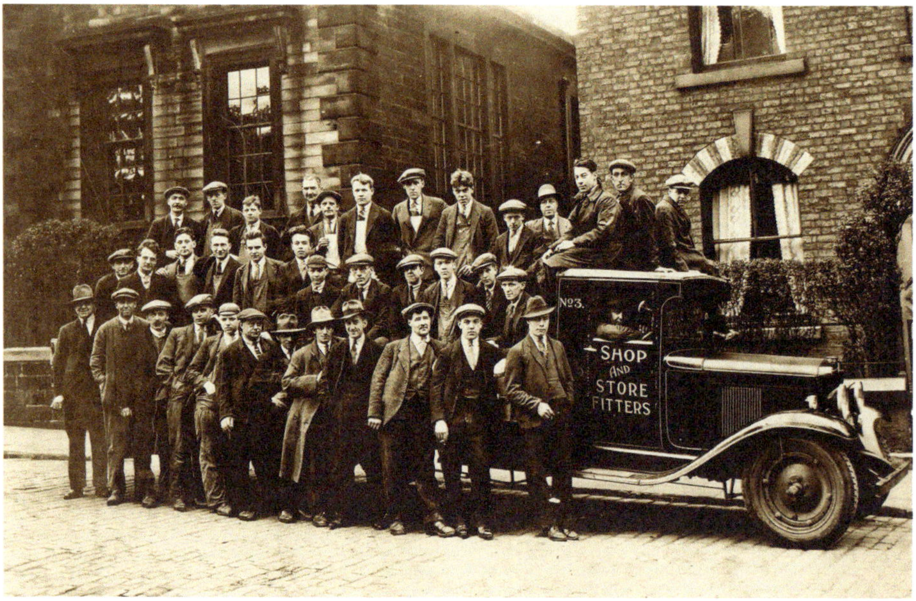

The lorry and staff of Drake & Warters Ltd in 1933 outside part of the company's premises on Thornhill Street.

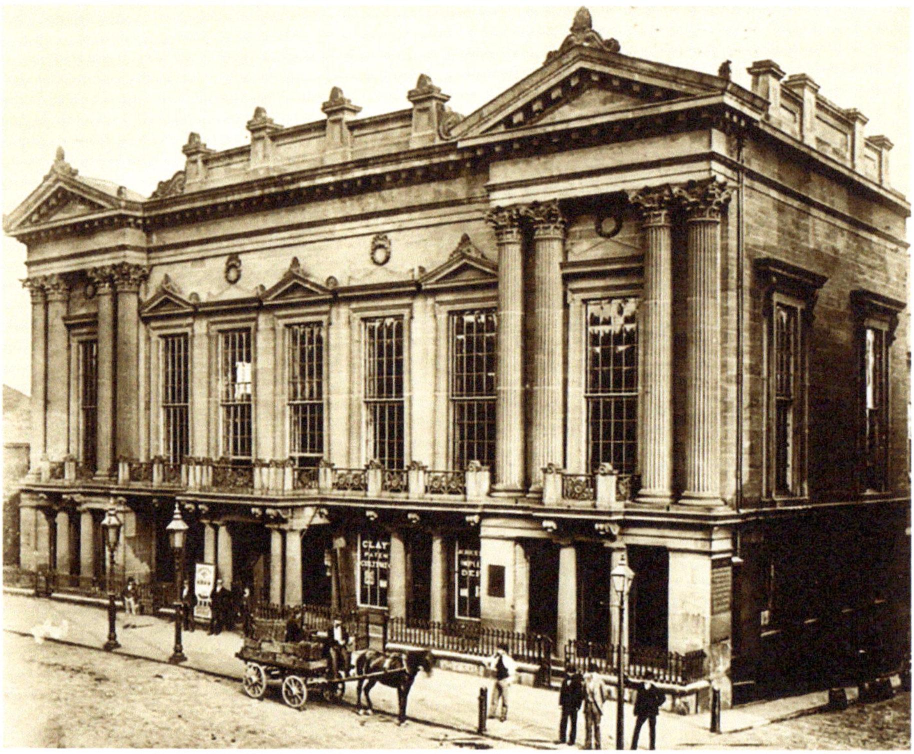

One of the most accomplished of all of Wakefield's grand civic buildings was the Corn Exchange, which was opened in 1838.

As well as a nationally important trade in corn and wool, Wakefield also boasted a large trade in livestock. Such was the scale of the business that by 1860 the cattle market was said to be the largest in the north of England, and perhaps Europe. The cattle market had been established in 1765 and on an average day in 1802 some 6,000 sheep and 800 cows were sold. The cattle market closed in the 1960s, but its legacy lives on with the road name Fair Ground Road. The scale of cattle selling was so great that any land suitable for grazing in the immediate environs of the town were turned over to fatten up the cattle before being sold at the market. This raised the price of the land to such a premium, as did the need for huge tracts of land for tentering cloth, that it made industrial development un-economical.

Music, particularly church music was a Wakefield speciality for a time through building pipe organs for church, chapels and private houses. Established in the 1820s by Joseph Booth, the pipe organ building concern of Booth & Co. flourished from 1824 through to 1893. The firm was established on Chestnut Lane in the 1830s, which was renamed Howard Street in the 1850s. The large purpose-built factory was over three floors. Led by Booth from 1830 to his death in 1874, the firm built pipe organs across the globe: shipping an organ to Napoleon III in Biarritz, France, and no less than seventeen to the Caribbean. By 1874 a second organ building factory had been established on Clarion Street: Belle Vue, by Joseph Hepworth. Indeed, he built Clarion Street and nearby Elm Tree Street. A third concern was managed by Alfred Kirkland in the Old Town Hall on Crown Court, Wood Street, and a fourth was set up by John Valentine Marshall. Today, Andrew Carter of Canal Street keeps the tradition alive. At one point an organ by Booth & Co. could be found in nearly all of Wakefield's various churches and chapels: West Parade Wesleyan Chapel, Market Street United Methodist Church, Parish Church of St Michael the Archangel, Holy Trinity George Street, Zion Independent Chapel, Salem Independent Chapel, and Wakefield Cathedral. Just one instrument remains: that built in 1874 in Westgate Chapel.

The railways had been a major employer. The large shed at Belle Vue, 25A, up to the 1960s had employed hundreds of men. The shed, which had an allocation of over 120 locomotives in the 1950s, officially closed in June 1967. Part of the complex remained open for wagon repairs until 1983. The shed was demolished in 1993 and has been cleared for redevelopment in 2019. Close by to Wakefield was Ardsley Shed, the largest such establishment in the West Riding.

Greens Economiser works at Calder Vale were one of the largest employers in Wakefield and district. E. Greens of Wakefield patented their Economiser boilers in the 1840s. This is now recognised as a milestone in making eco-friendly fuel-efficient systems. Born and bred in Wakefield, Edward Green (1799–1865) is one of the city's most important innovators, and some of the principles of his landmark 1845 design are still used by the company in today's Economiser boilers. Consisting of a series of metal tubes, usually made from cast iron, the Economiser did exactly what its name suggested. It economised energy usage by using what would otherwise have been waste heat from boilers to heat up the feed water. The invention, an improvement on the basic steam engine designed by James Watt, was patented in 1845. It made a splash at the Great Exhibition at Crystal Palace in 1851 and was soon being used as far afield as Russia and North America. 'Old Neddy', as he became known, died in 1861, to be succeeded as head of what was now E. Green & Son by his son, also called Edward.

Edward Jr, who naturally earned the nickname 'Young Neddy', was elected Conservative MP for Wakefield, a position he retained for seven years. The company remained in the Green family until 1961. Green's became a household name in the twentieth century, and in 1912 George V opened the firm's new factory in Wakefield. In the 1950s Green's invented extended surface finned tubes and developed machinery to produce them. Investment continued to

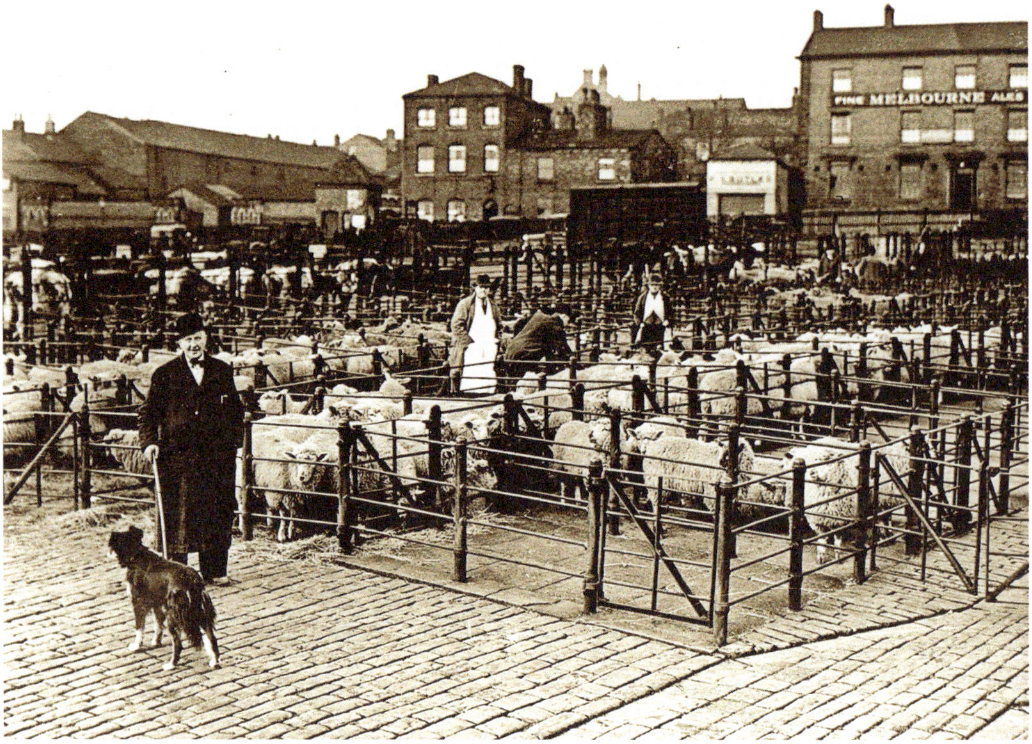

Above, below and next page: Several views of Wakefield's cattle market, once the largest in the north of England. The site became a timber store for Drake & Warters Ltd in the 1960s and 1970s. It is now occupied by the central sorting office for the Post Office in Wakefield.

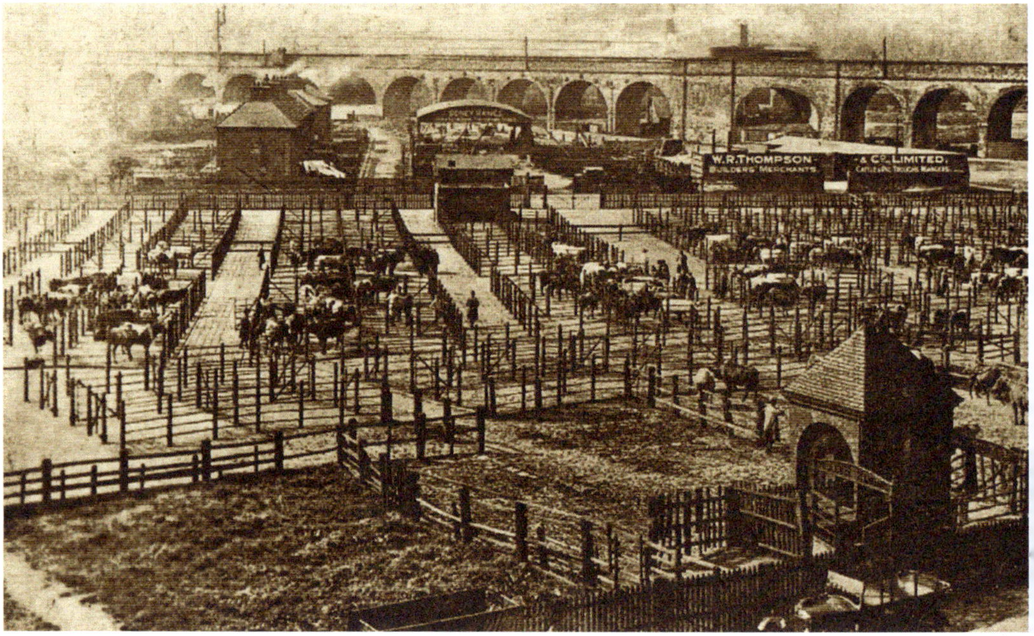

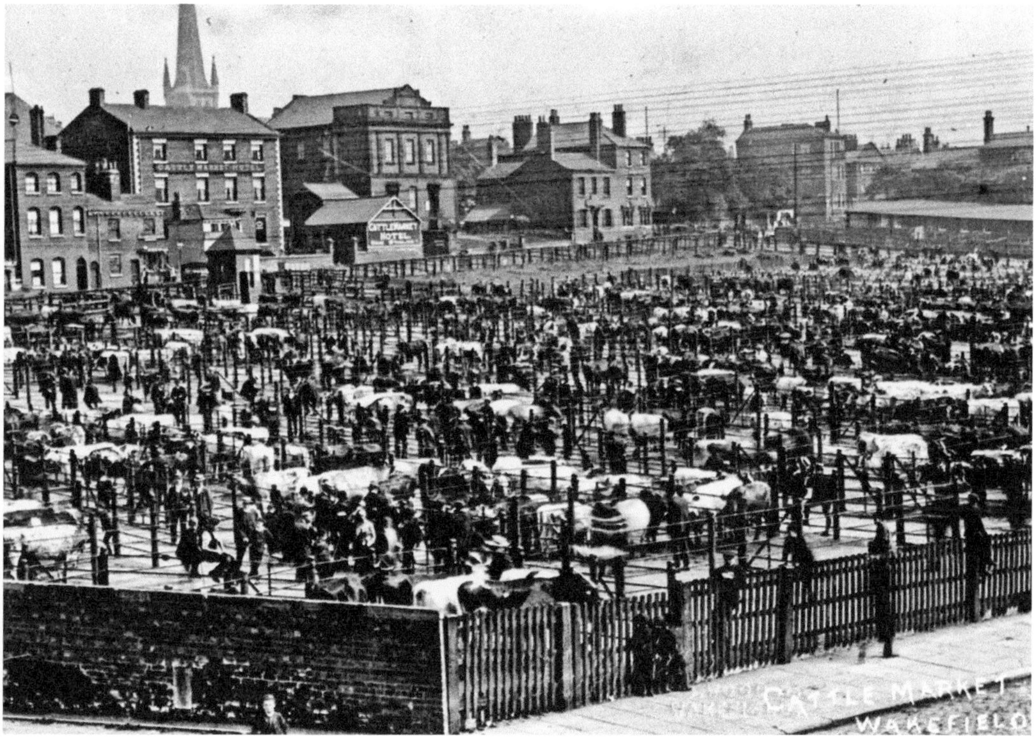
CATTLE MARKET HOTEL
CATTLE MARKET
WAKEFIELD

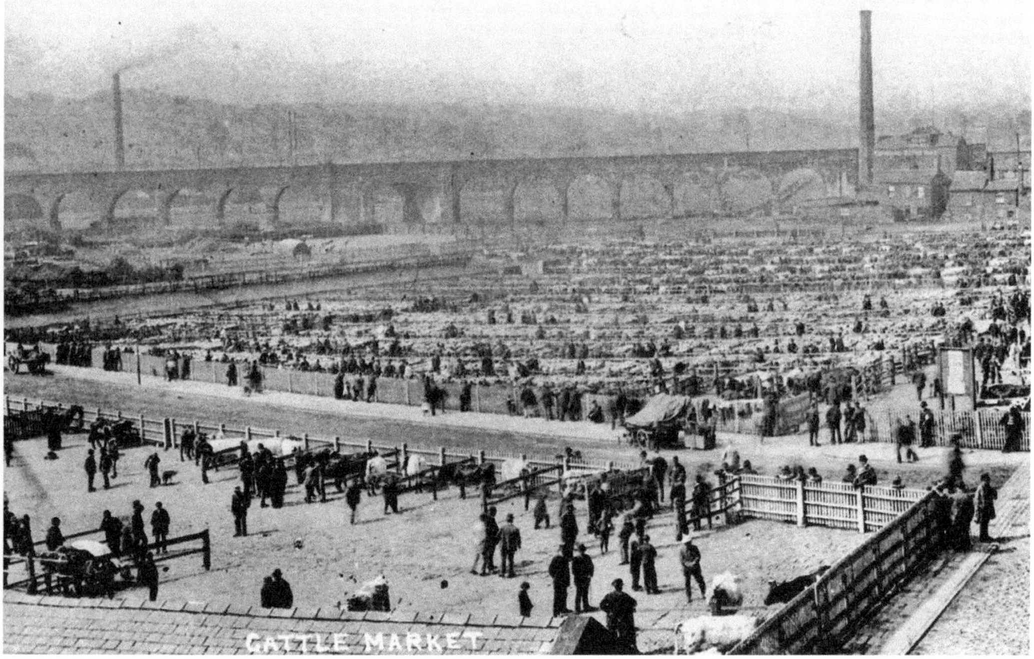
CATTLE MARKET

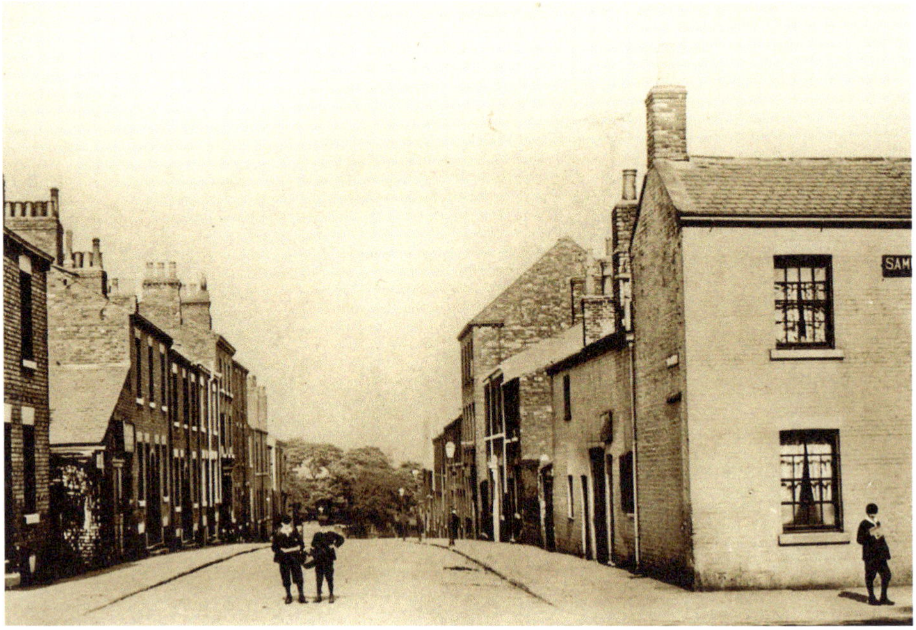

In the centre of the picture we see the large three-floor factory premises of Booth & Co., pipe organ builders. During the Second World War the factory was used for war purposes. It was demolished in the 1960s.

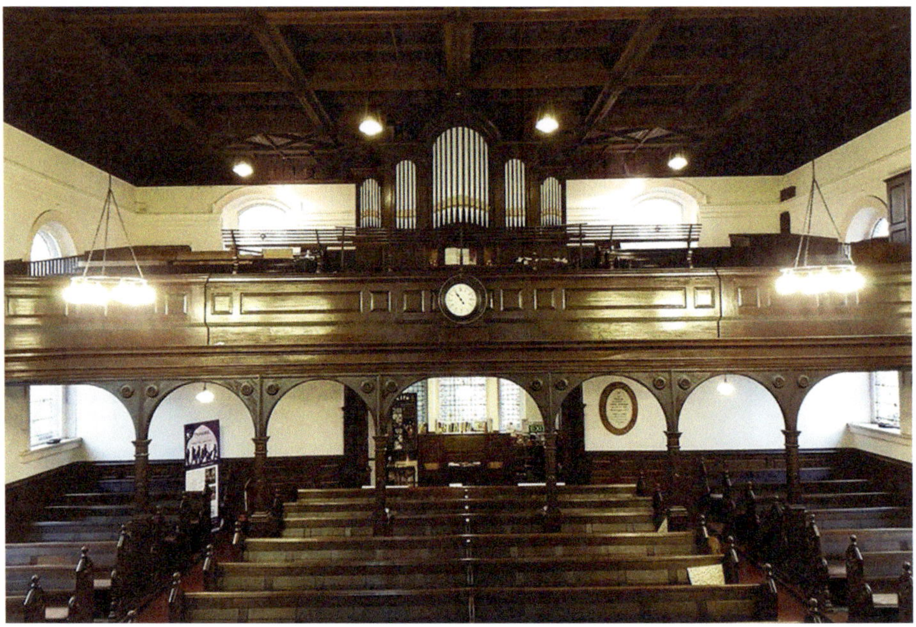

The last remaining pipe organ by Booth & Co. of Wakefield remaining in the city is housed in Westgate Chapel. It was completed in February 1874 during the ministry of Revd Goodwyn Barmby and was the last organ built by Francis Booth (1801–1874), who had attended the chapel between 1844 and 1858. His son, Henry, was a lifelong Unitarian.

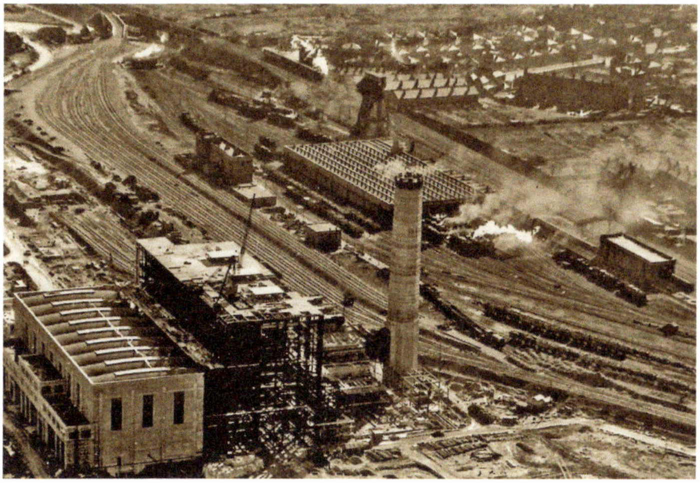

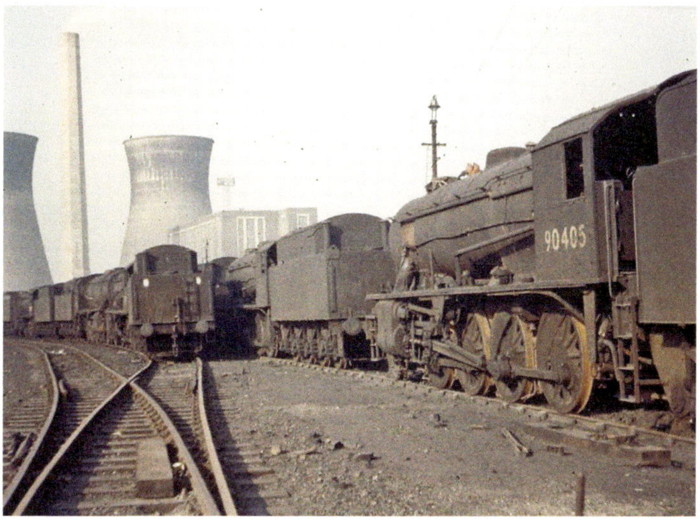

This page and next page: Five views of the vast engine shed at Belle Vue. Close by to the shed was Wakefield's very own – and no longer demolished – power station. In several shots we can see the lines of engines to be sent to the scrap man in the 1960s during the run down of steam traction.

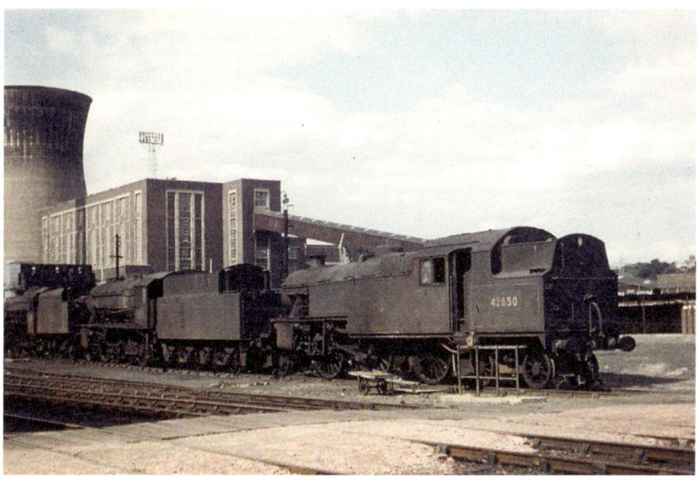

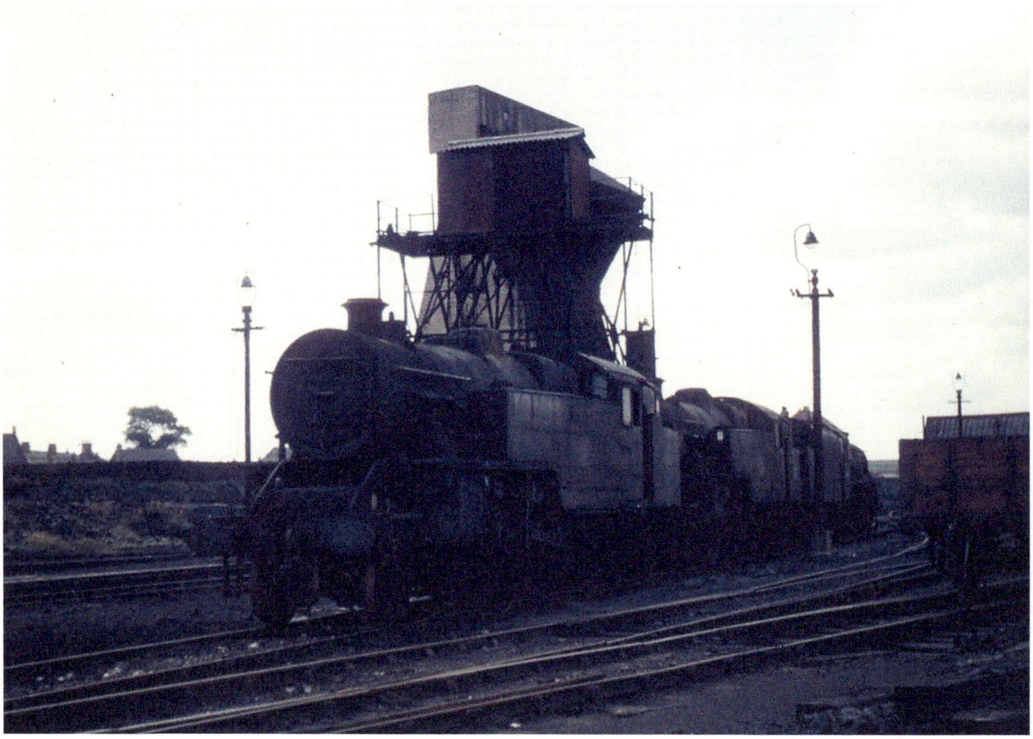

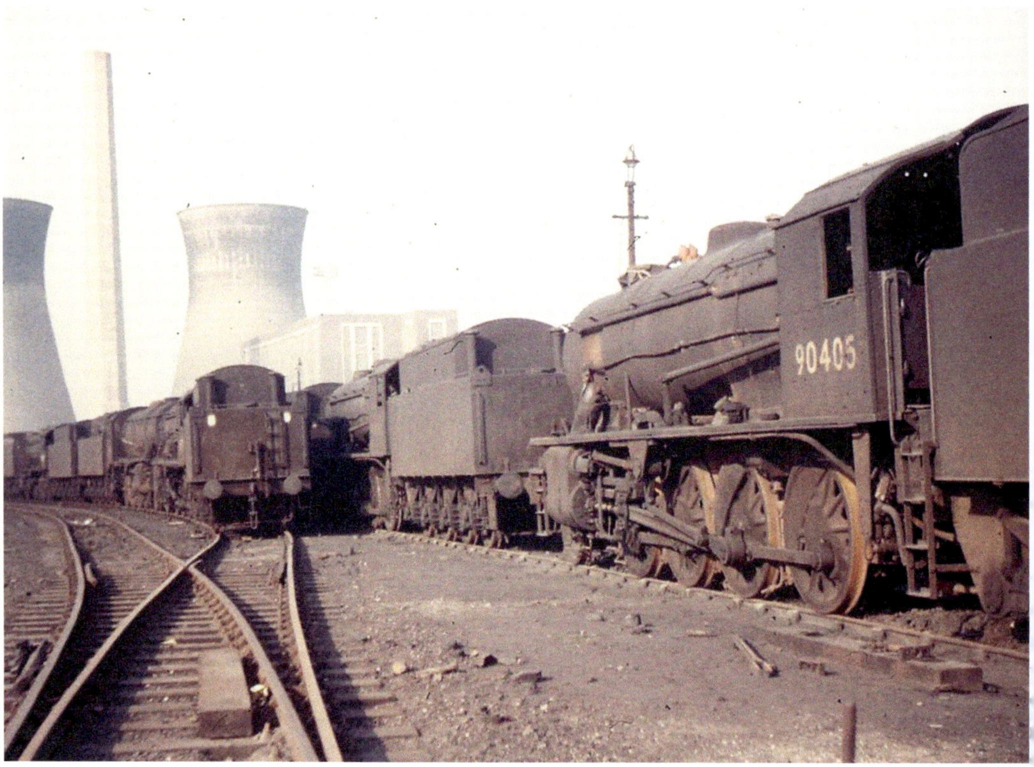
90405

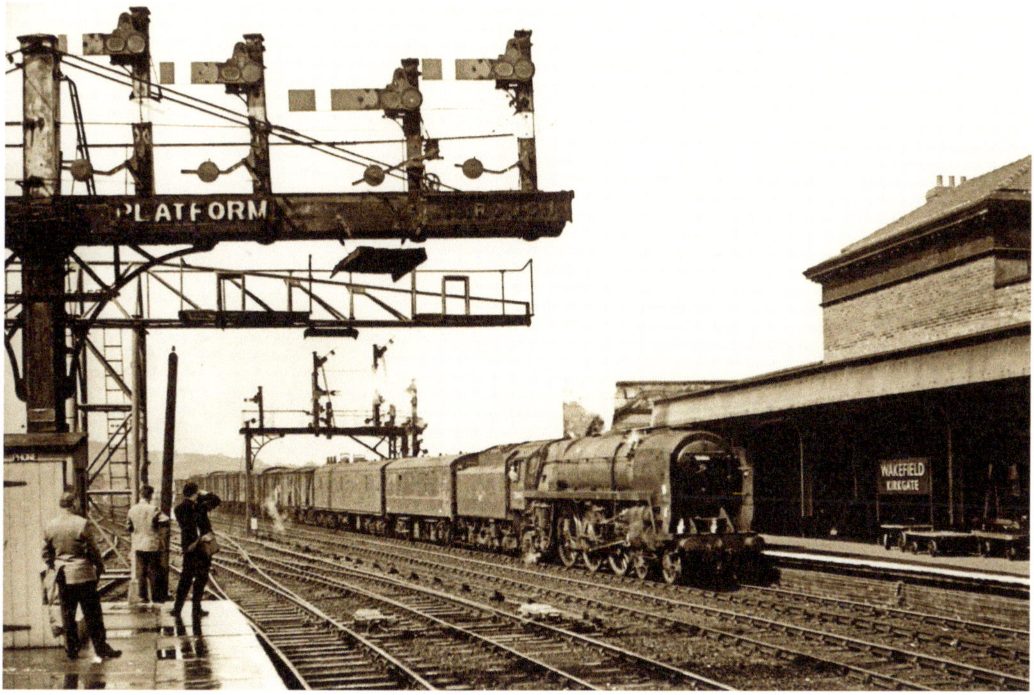

Above, below and next page: Wakefield from 1840 was linked to the then developing railway with the opening of Kirkgate station on 5 October 1840.

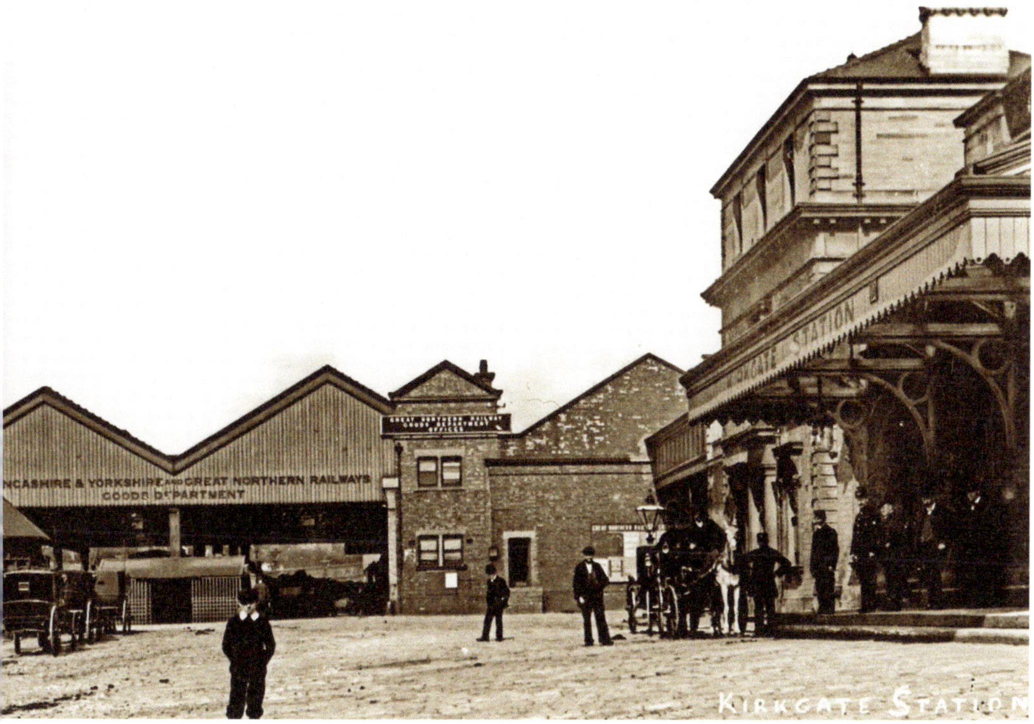

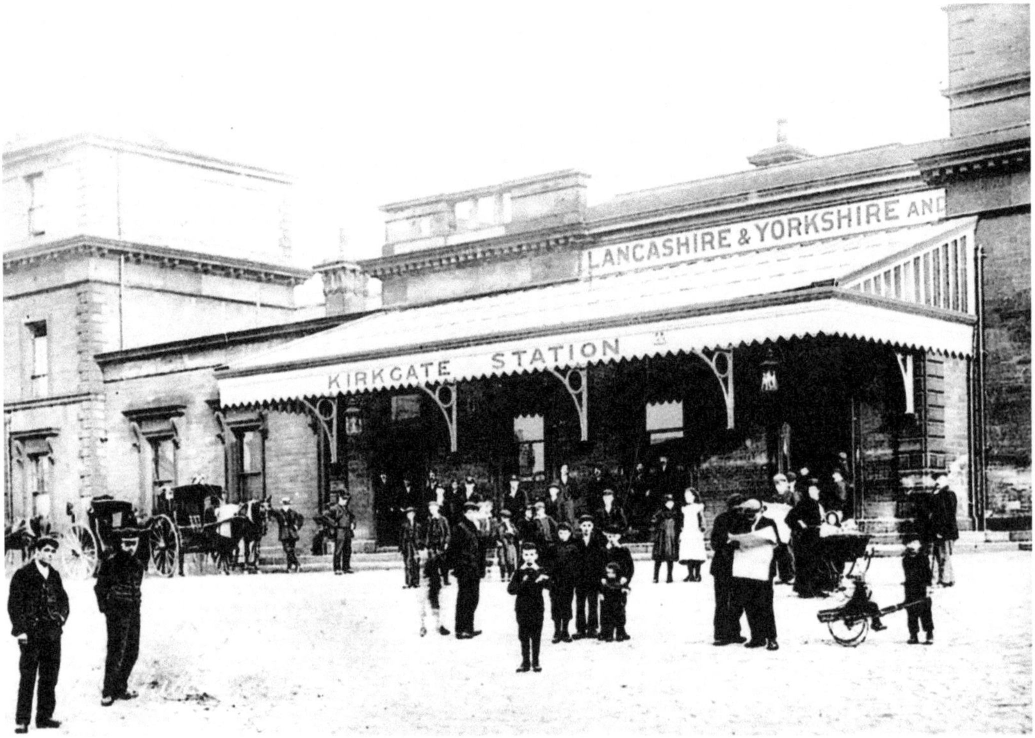
LANCASHIRE & YORKSHIRE AND
KIRKGATE STATION

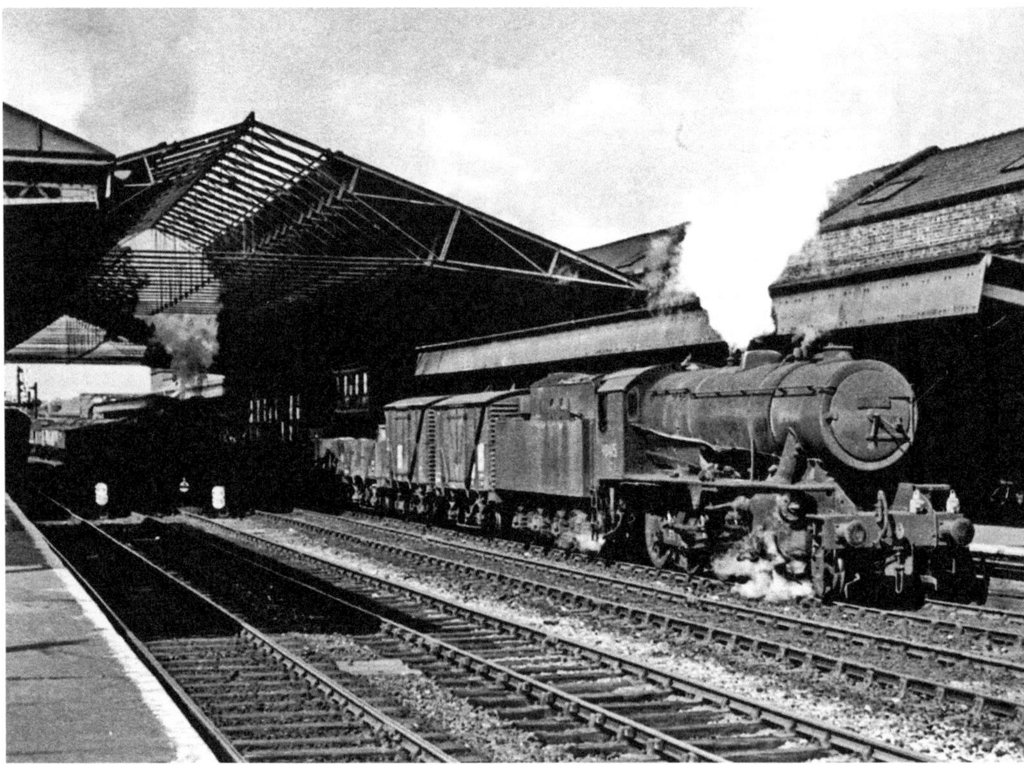

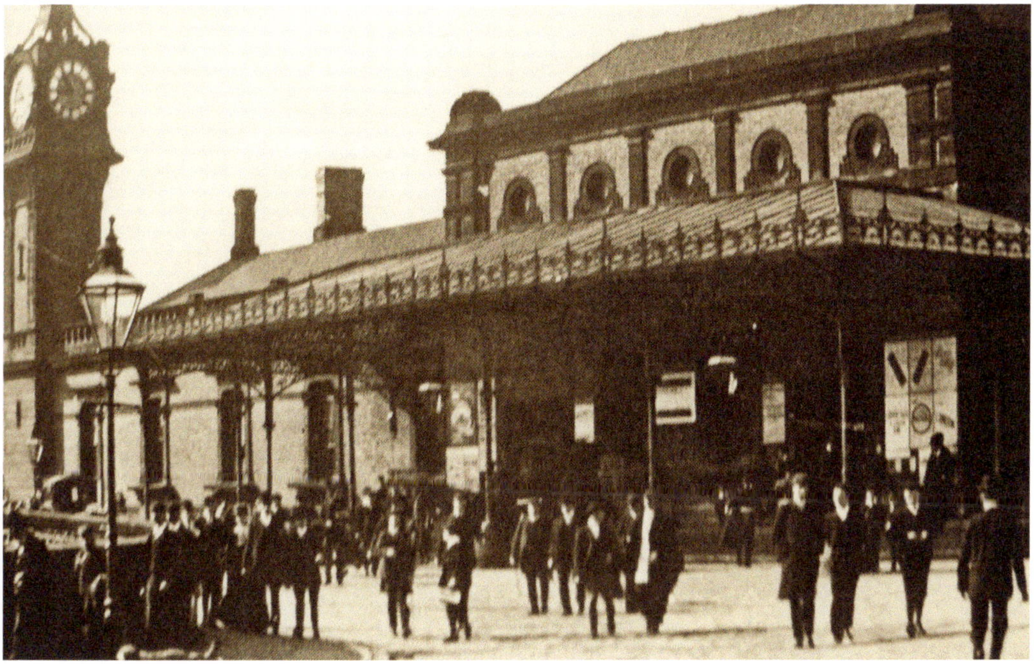

Westgate station clock tower dominated the cityscape until the 1960s and can be seen here in all its former glory. The station opened in 1867, replacing one that had stood virtually opposite that had been opened in 1857 when the line was completed.

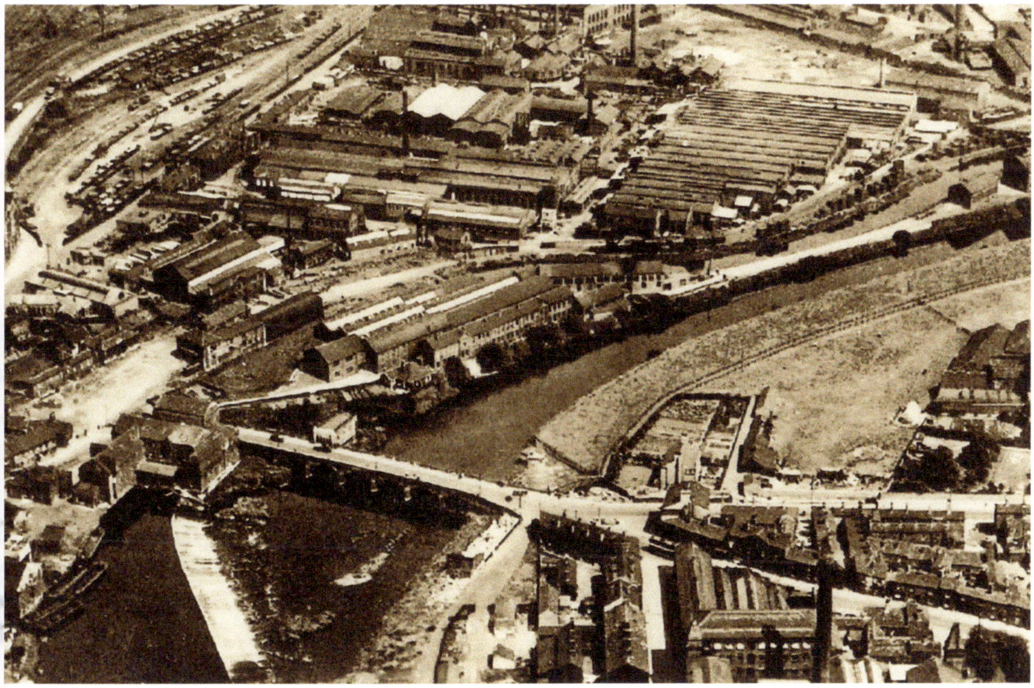

An aerial view of E. Green & Sons Economiser Works at Calder Vale.

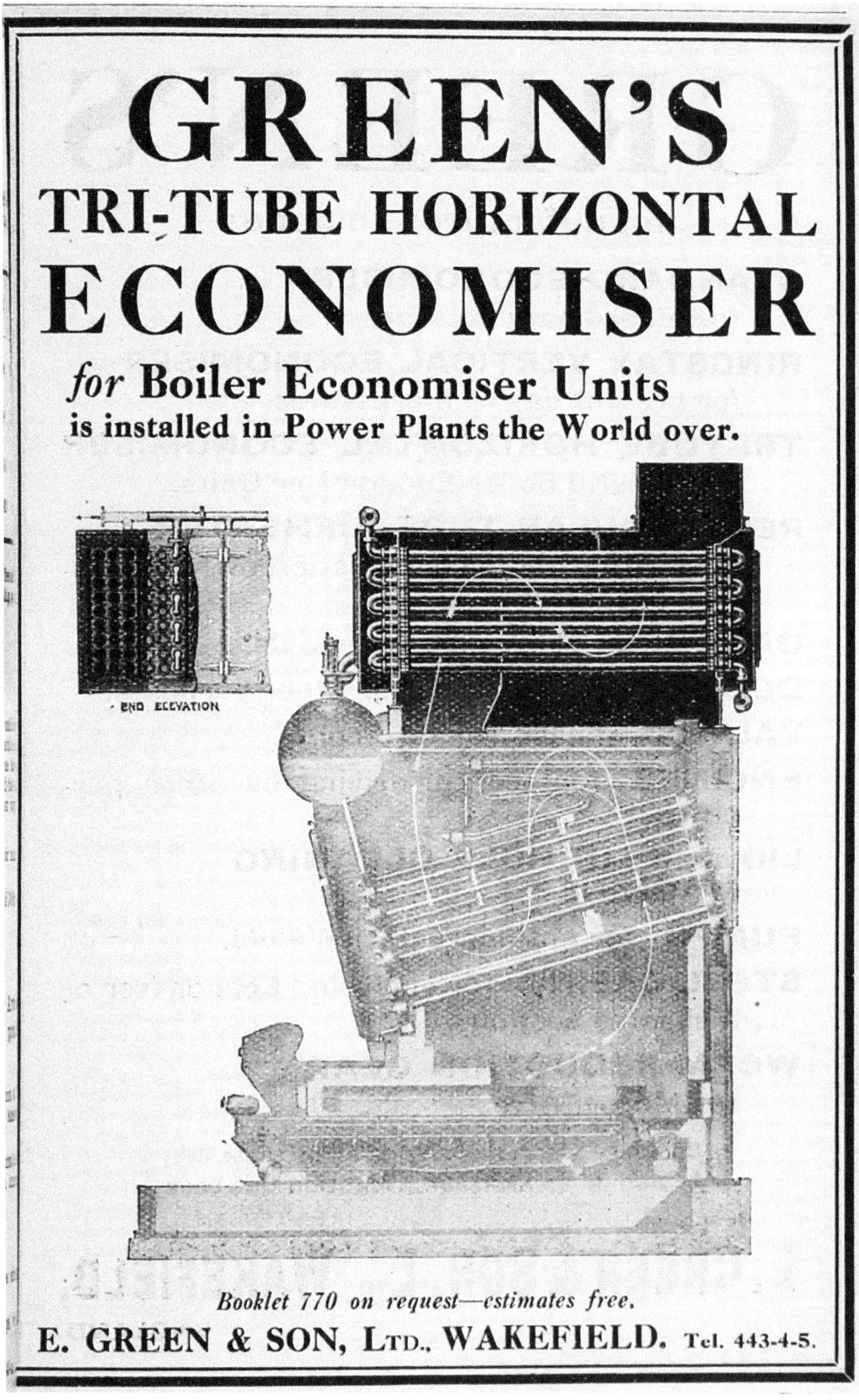

An advertisement for E. Green & Sons.

refine the design and optimise product performance. The firm continues to flourish from its Wakefield factory.

A thriving Wakefield company is Group Rhodes. In 1824, Joseph Rhodes, as a young man of twenty, built his first machine in a small workshop in Wakefield. From making machines to turn out such items as cutlery and oil cans for households in the West Yorkshire town, the company has progressed to designing high-tech computer-controlled machine tools for worldwide distribution. And, as Joseph Rhodes was way ahead of his time, the company still follows that pioneering spirit of invention and innovation.

In 1899 Joseph Rhodes & Sons became a limited company and registered the Colossus of Rhodes as its trademark. Some twenty-two years later the company expanded into its present 8-acre site at Belle Vue, Wakefield. The new factory provided an ideal platform for the company's continued growth.

Joseph Rhodes had entered the export market early in its history, opening an office in Paris as early as 1910, but exports increased sharply after the Second World War, particularly to Europe and the USA. In the 1950s the export drive was further assisted by Rhodes's invention of the world's first hydraulic shear and press brake, which received patent protection in 1943.

A series of innovative products rapidly followed the introduction of the hydraulic shear, including the stagger feed press for the production of tin plate as canister lids and shoe polish tins, and the impact extrusion press used in the forming of battery casings and toothpaste tubes, which has proved particularly successful. By the mid-1950s the company could boast a product range of thousands of types of machines for the sheet metal working industry. The *British Machine Tool Engineering Magazine* for March 1954 claimed such a range to be 'the largest variety made by any firm in the world'. Group Rhodes came into being in 2001 and is renowned for supplying high-quality, state-of-the-art machinery.

Another major employer in Wakefield was British Ropes. British Ropes was company established on 6 June 1924 through the merger of eight companies, which included George Craddock & Co. of Wakefield. George Cradock & Co. Ltd was originally founded in Darlington and moved to Wakefield in 1853. The firm originally produced hemp rope, but moved into wire rope in 1854 and the company went from strength to strength. In 1885 machinery was installed for the drawing of its own wire and an extensive steel works were erected in 1899 for the manufacture of their own steel. The company manufactured wire ropes from the raw material to the finished article and was the only works in Britain to do this at the time. The Wakefield premises were on Thornes Road and were demolished in the early 1990s to make way for Cathedral Retail Park, a new multiplex cinema, housing and other leisure outlets.

Another lost company was Bradley & Craven. This was a manufacturing company specialising in brickmaking machinery in Wakefield. It was founded in 1843 by two young engineers, William Craven and Richard Bradley, to manufacture what was then revolutionary machinery for automating clay brick production. Their 1853 patented 'Stiff-Plastic Brickmaking Machine' in combination with the Hoffman continuous kiln were responsible for changes in the industry that eventually saw a shift from hand craft to mechanised production. Their machines were manufactured at the Westgate Common Foundry in Wakefield and were sold throughout the United Kingdom as well as many overseas markets such as Australia, South Africa and Germany. The company also made steam engines, colliery winding gear and exhibited in the 1862 London International Exhibition. In 1972 Bradley & Craven, amalgamated with a rival Leeds company, Thomas C. Fawcett, forming Craven Fawcett Ltd, and was dissolved in 2002. The factory premises on Dewsbury Road were demolished to make way for car showrooms.

WIRE ROPE WORKS AT WAKEFIELD

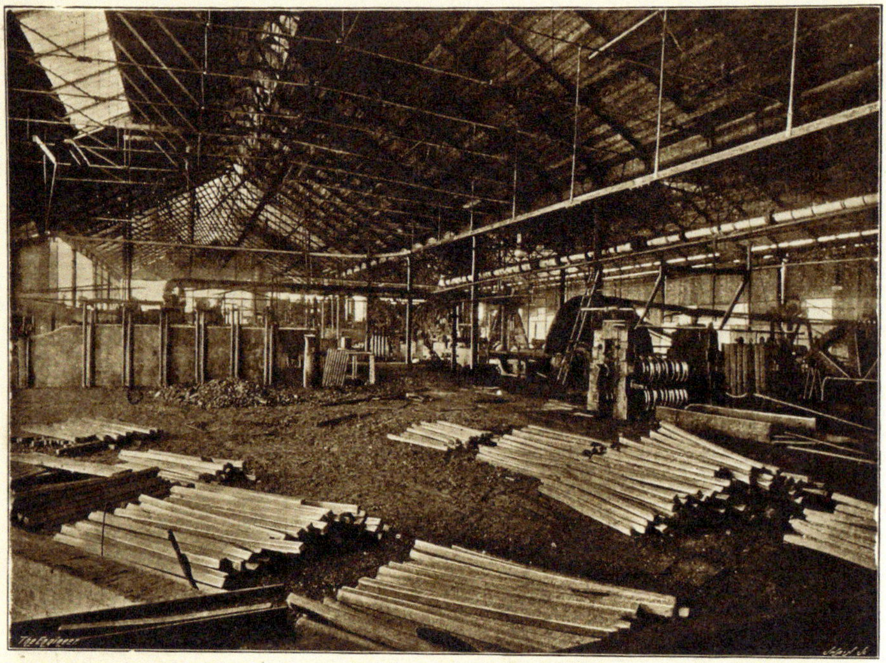

GENERAL VIEW OF STEEL WORKS

WIRE ROPE WORKS

MESSRS. GEORGE CRADOCK AND COMPANY, WAKEFIELD, ENGINEERS

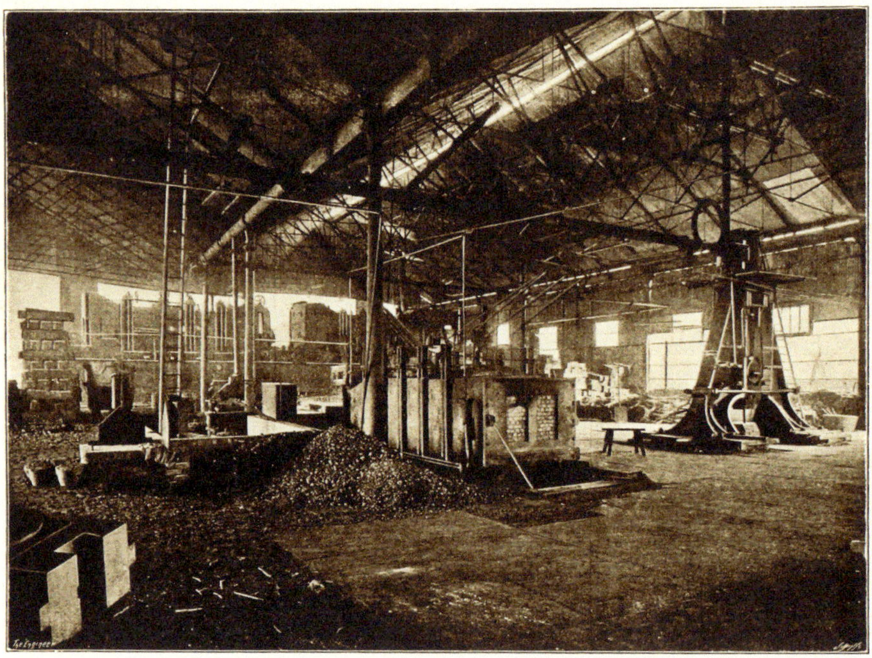

RE-HEATING FURNACE AND STEAM HAMMER

WIRE ROPE WORKS

MESSRS. GEORGE CRADOCK AND COMPANY, WAKEFIELD, ENGINEERS

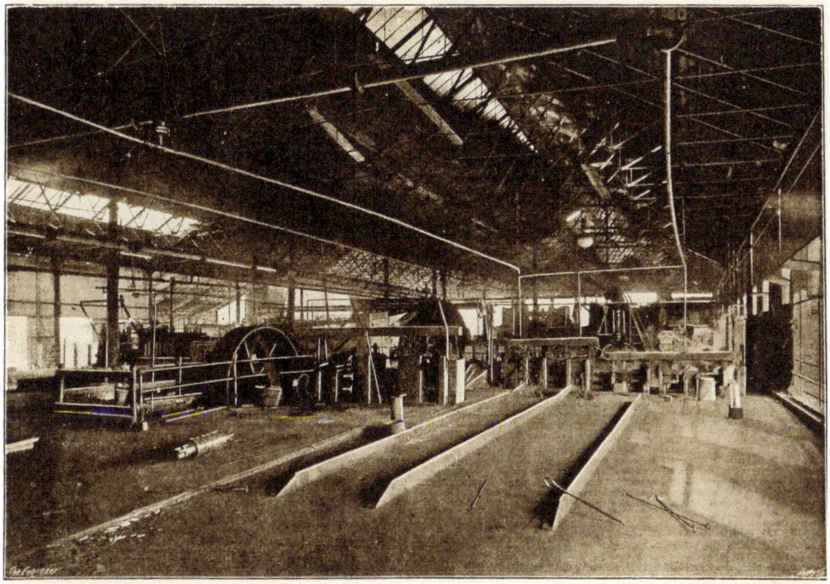

THE ROLLING MILLS

This page, previews page and next page: Craddocks rope works on Denby Dale Road was once a major employer in the city; it was latterly known as British Ropes. Here we see several views inside the vast factory in the years before the First World War. The factory is now the site of B&Q and a huge retail park that includes a multiplex cinema and numerous restaurants.

WIRE ROPE WORKS AT WAKEFIELD—LAYING SHOP

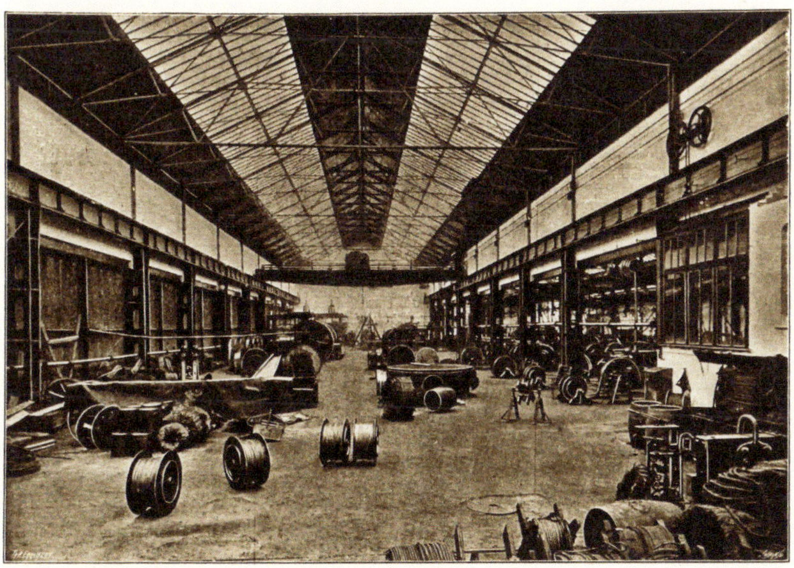

WIRE ROPE WORKS

MESSRS. GEORGE CRADOCK AND COMPANY, WAKEFIELD, ENGINEERS

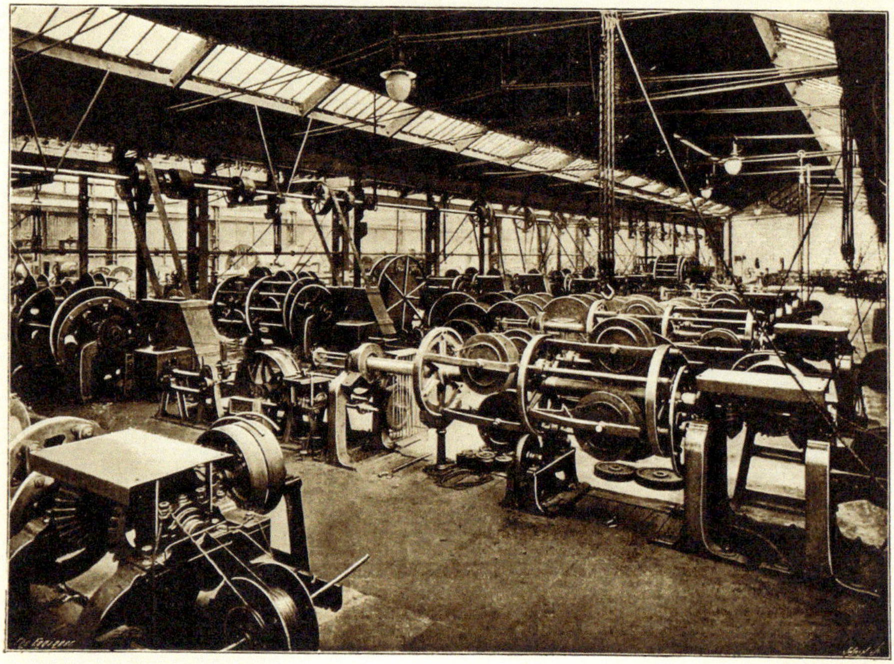

THE STRANDING SHOP

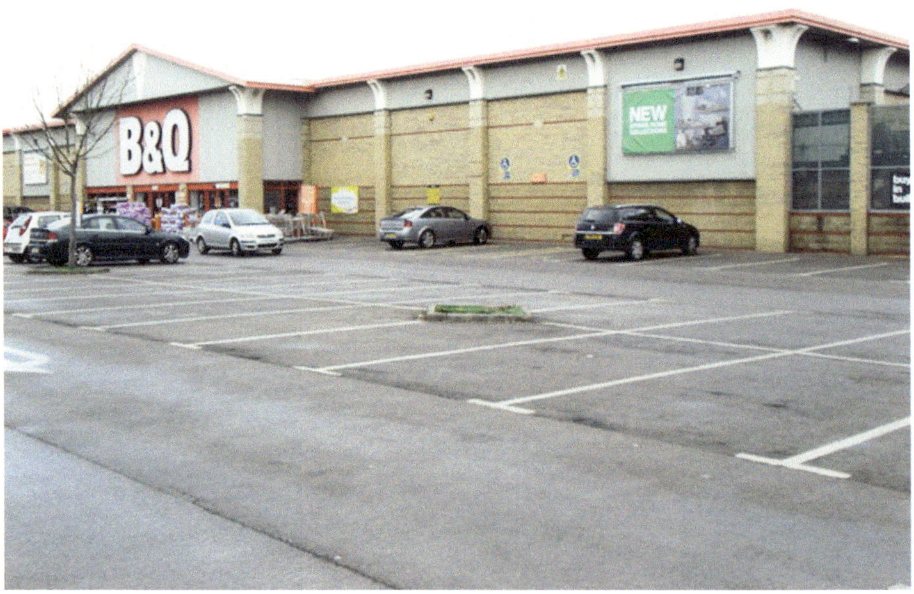

WIRE ROPE WORKS

MESSRS. GEORGE CRADOCK AND COMPANY, WAKEFIELD, ENGINEERS

(*For description see page 98*)

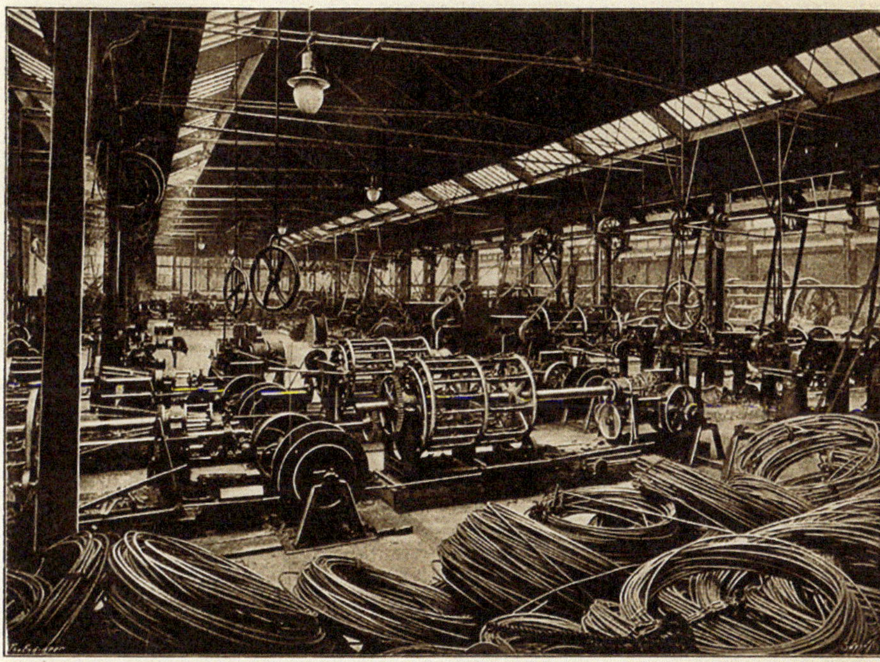

THE STRANDING SHOP

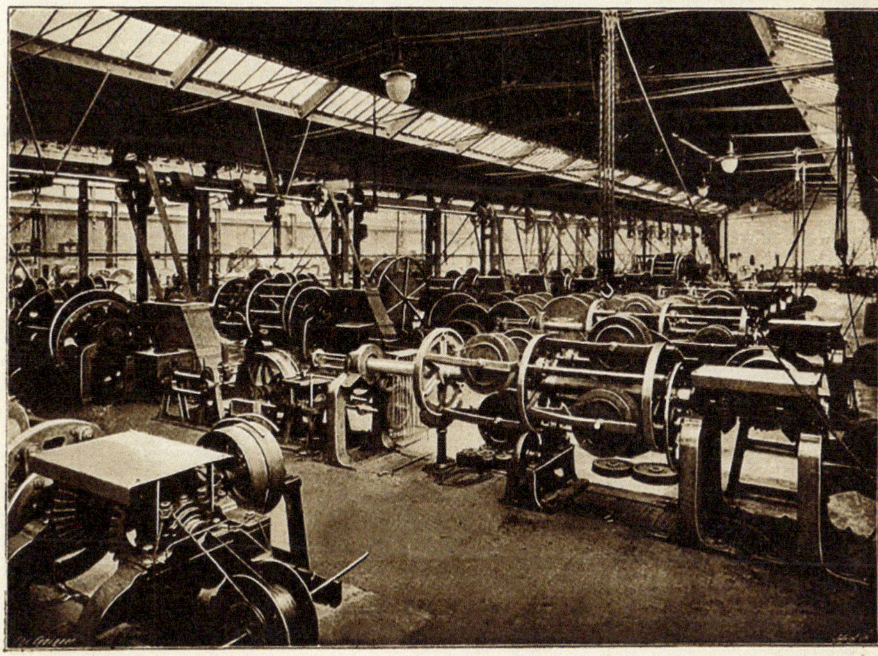

THE STRANDING SHOP

George Craddock & Co. wire rope works.

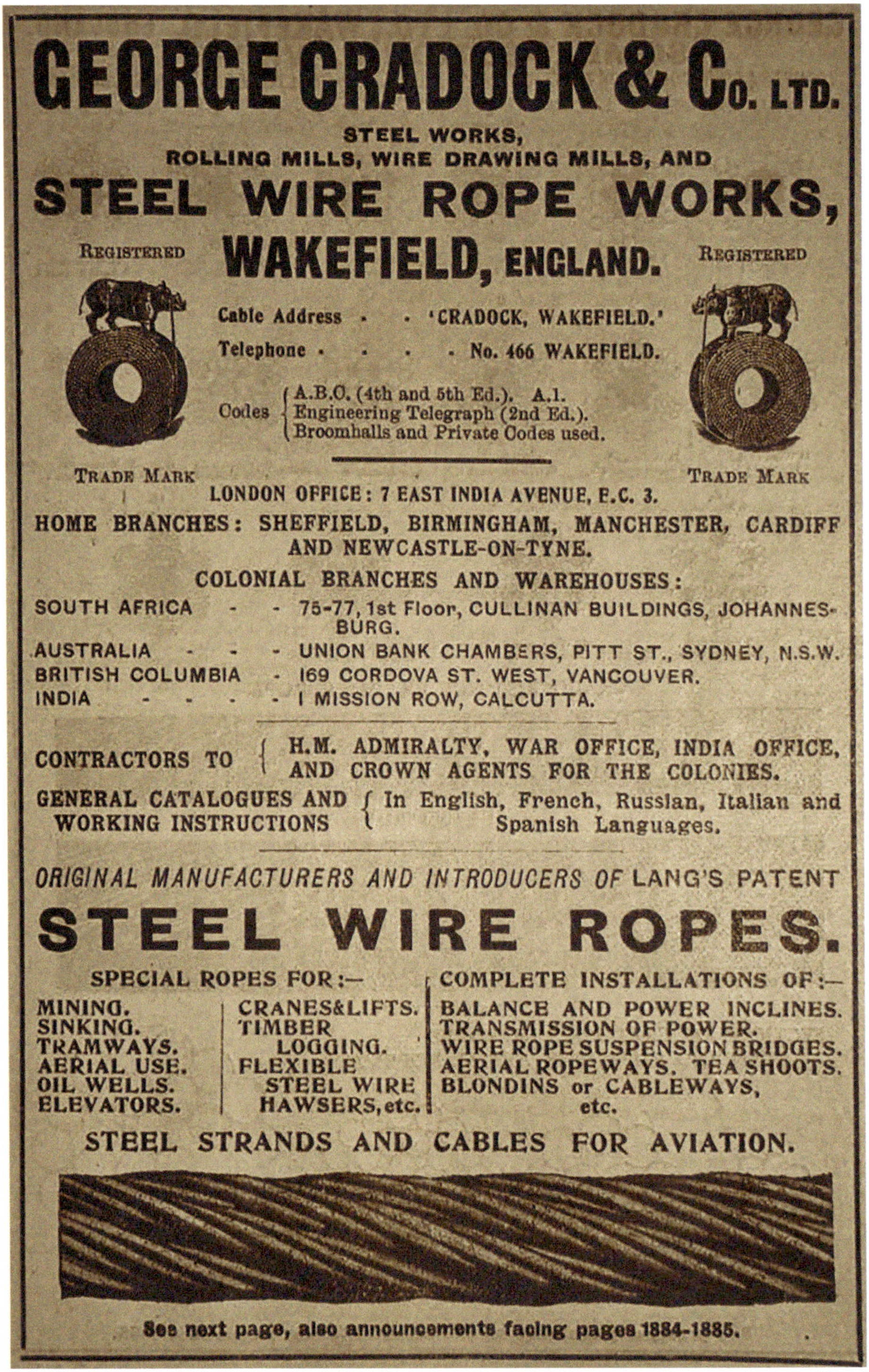

An advert for Craddocks ropes. The factory site was cleared in the early 1990s to make way for a retail park.

Many may remember Beverley Brother's ales. It was founded in 1861, having 173 tied houses from Lancashire to Teesside. The firm was taken over by Watney Mann's Wilsons operation in March 1967, with the usual promise of no redundancies, and closed in October 1968. After the closure of the brewery, the Wines and Spirits Distribution Plant was kept going until 1971. Much of the site is now occupied by a new health centre, and Fernandes' Old Malt House was once Beverleys' malthouse.

Today Wakefield is a major retail centre. The Ridings Shopping Centre and Trinity Walk are two large shopping center developments. The site of British Ropes factory on Denby Dale Road is now developed as Cathedral Retail Park. MP Stonehouse's factory was demolished in 1989 and replaced with another retail park. The Mines Rescue Station on Ings Road was swept away in the 1990s to make way for strip mall development stretching from Denby Dale Road to Kirkgate. Wakefield in 2020 shows little sign of its once proud textile, mining and engineering past. Nor does the modern city wear its past: wholesale demolition in the 1950s to 1970s destroyed hundreds, if not thousands, of precious, irreplaceable, historic buildings. Wakefield's wealth was built on wool, which for a time Wakefield and the Milnes family of Westgate Chapel dominated. Clayton Hospital, a fine neo-Gothic building built by Daniel Gaskell as a memorial for his wife, will be swept away for humdrum modern architecture, severing a link to the past. Once these buildings are gone they can never be replaced. Daniel Gaskell and his Unitarian antecedents did much to make Wakefield the capital of the West

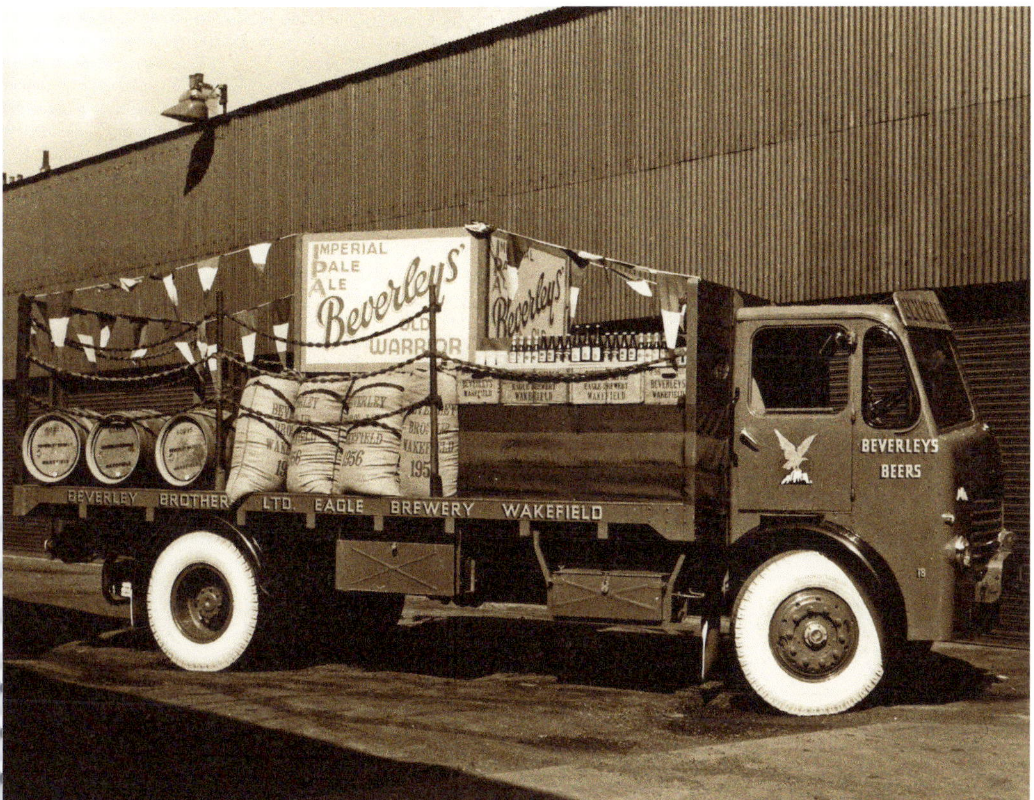

Beverleys' Brewer lorry. Many will remember these distinctive lorries on their rounds delivery to local pubs controlled by the brewery – notably the Griffin Hotel on Union Street.

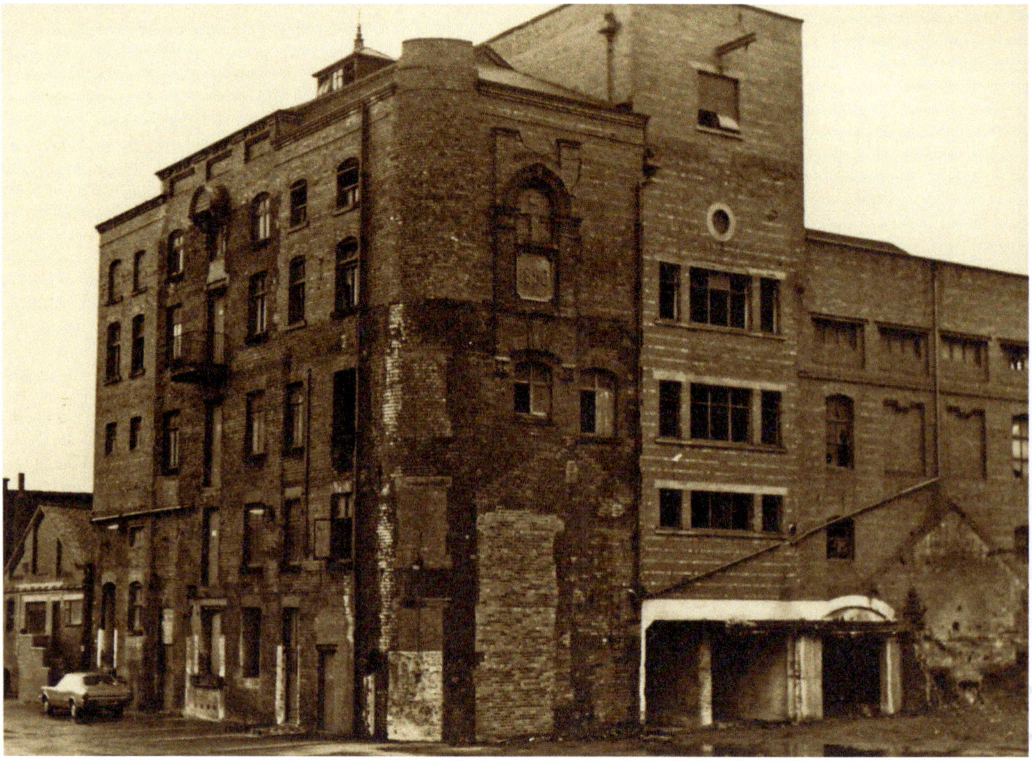

Above, below and next page: Beverleys' Brewer off Thorn Hill Street was a well-known local landmark for well over 100 years. It was demolished to make way for the Medical Trinity Centre. We see a works outing as well as the factory gates just after the Second World War.

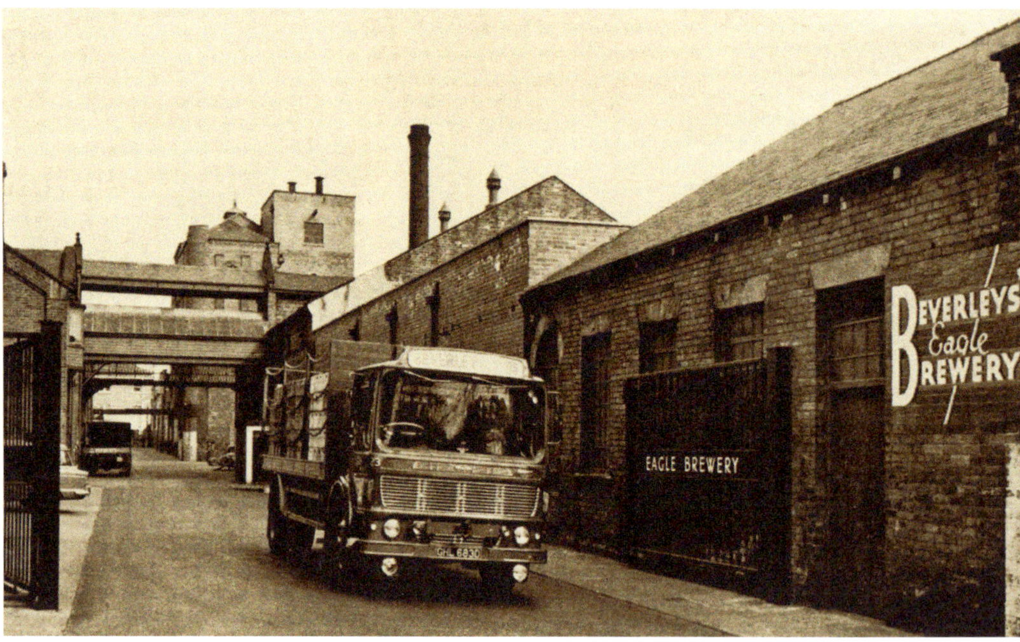

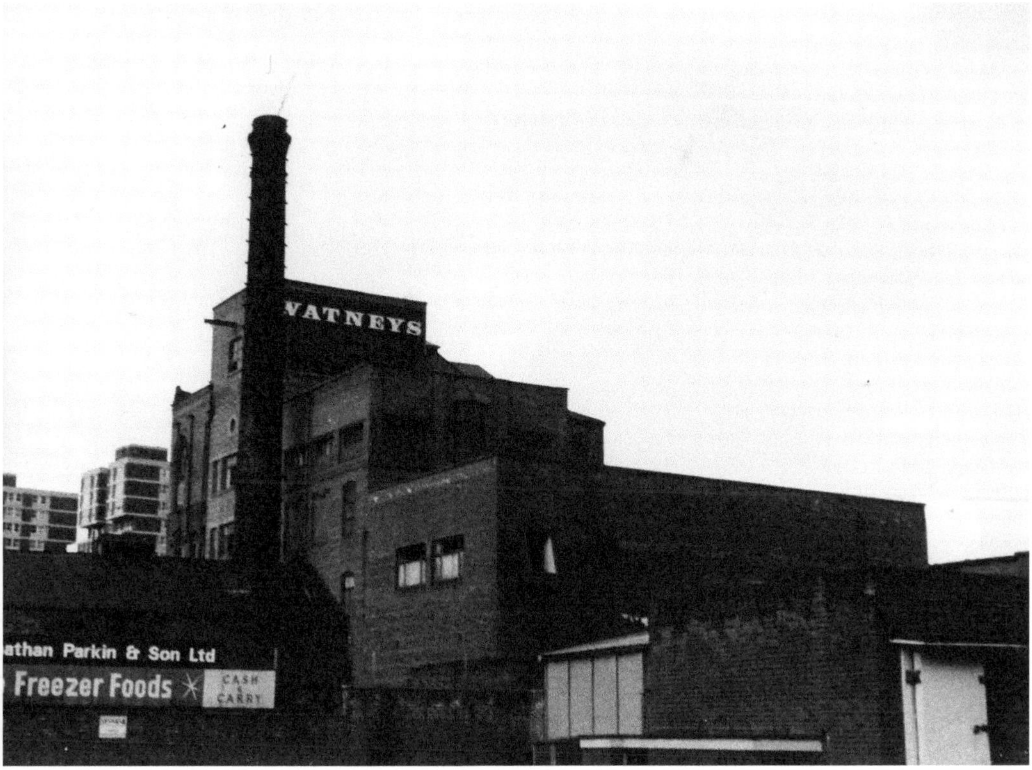
WATNEYS
athan Parkin & Son Ltd
Freezer Foods
CASH & CARRY

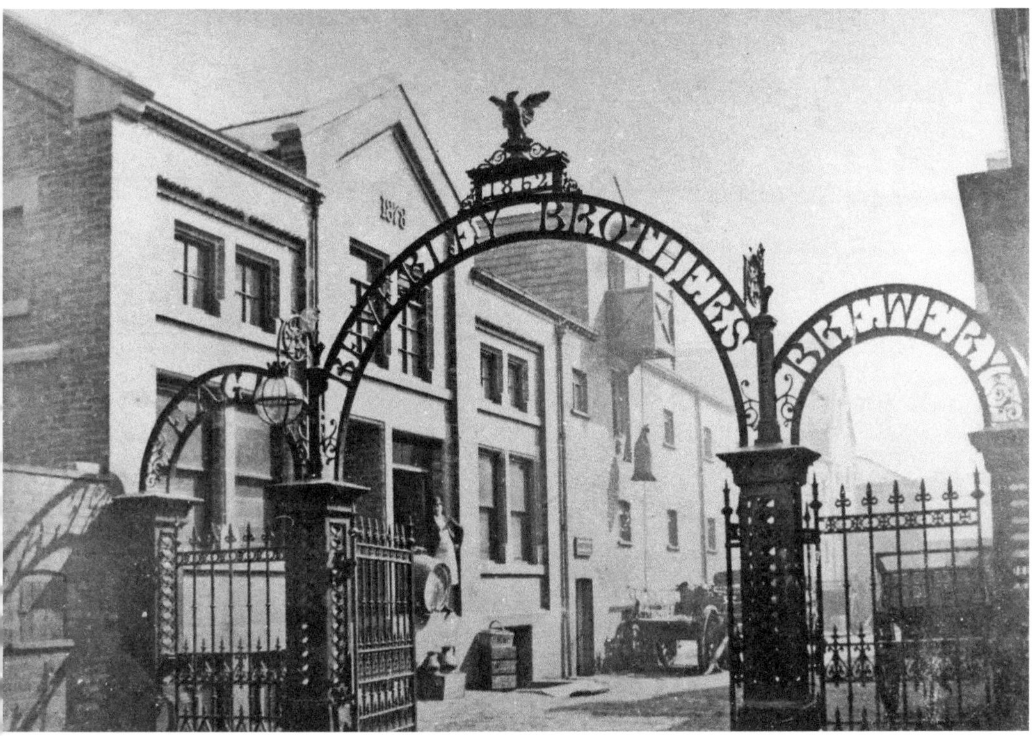
1852
BROTHERS
BREWERY

Riding. Between 1700 and 1830 Westgate Chapel men and women had led the development of wool trade in Wakefield and area. They had invested capital in building steam-powered mills. Without the major investment by Unitarians, the cloth trade in Wakefield would have stagnated long before it did. By the 1840s the cloth trade was in a state of major change. The majority of wool cloth made before 1830 was produced on handlooms, and by the middle decades of the century steam-powered power looms had taken over. The woollen industry was slow to follow the lead set by cotton. After 1830 the economy of Wakefield had migrated from cloth and wool merchanting to worsted spinning with the concerns of George Lee & Son, M. P. Stonehouse's, Alfred Haley, Paton & Baldwin, and Rawson's to name but a few. These were supplemented by coal and heavy industry, with Park Hill pit, Greens Economiser Works, Westgate and Belle Vue Engine sheds being a few examples that we have looked at. As a child I remember the M. P. Stonehouse vast works on Ings Road and its tall imposing chimney, Alfred Haley's equally vast complex, the brooding bulk of the city's own power station, the pithead wheels, the miners and their bands marching through the city. Yet what remains? Is Wakefield intent on forgetting its own past? The city seems to have been cleansed of its industrial past. In neighbouring towns mills became shops and homes; not so Wakefield, which unhesitatingly demolished the mills to make way for now semi-derelict retail parks. Surely Stonehouse's mill could have been saved and converted? Likewise, Alfred Haley's complex or Patton & Baldwins'? Where are the memorials to the working men and women of Wakefield? Or the modern-day chartists? Where are the blue plaques to the loom workers? The tributes to the child labourers? We have plaques to the well off, the middle class, the affluent, but not to the workers that made these people wealthy. This book, I hope, has brought some of this forgotten legacy back to life in a small way, and shown the debt the city owes to its working men and women.

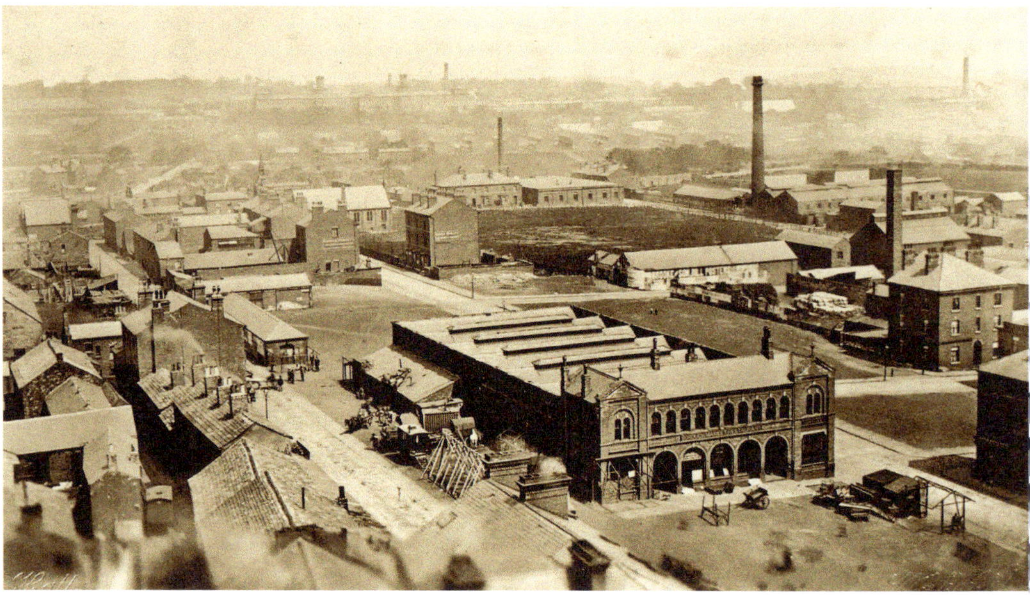

Wakefield Market was once the pride and joy of the city. It moved from Cross Square to new purpose-built premises in 1866. Here we see the new Borough Market building in 1880. It was demolished in the early years of the current century to make way for Trinity Walk shopping centre.

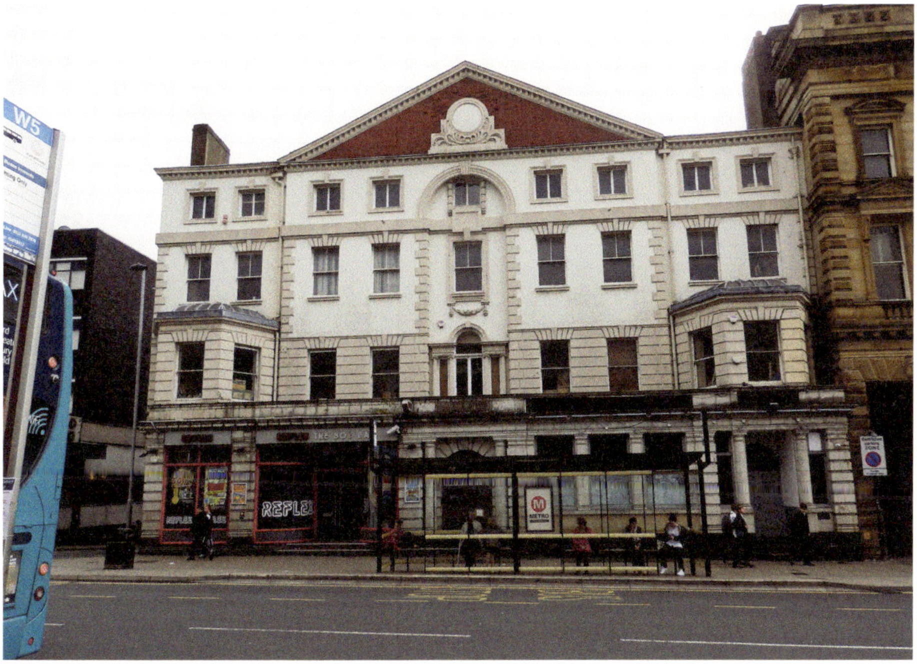

The Great Black Bull Hotel, once a thriving coaching inn, has developed into a dynamic art space for community use as well as several nightclubs. Wakefield became infamous as a destination for a night out from the late 1980s to early part of the current century.

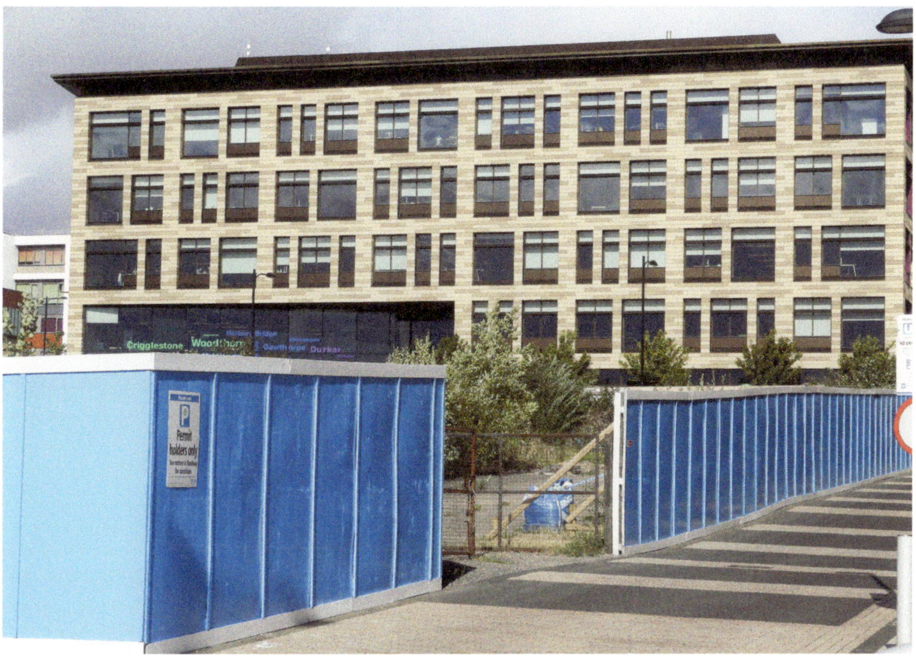

Wakefield One houses the offices and ancillary services of Wakefield Council, providing jobs for many.

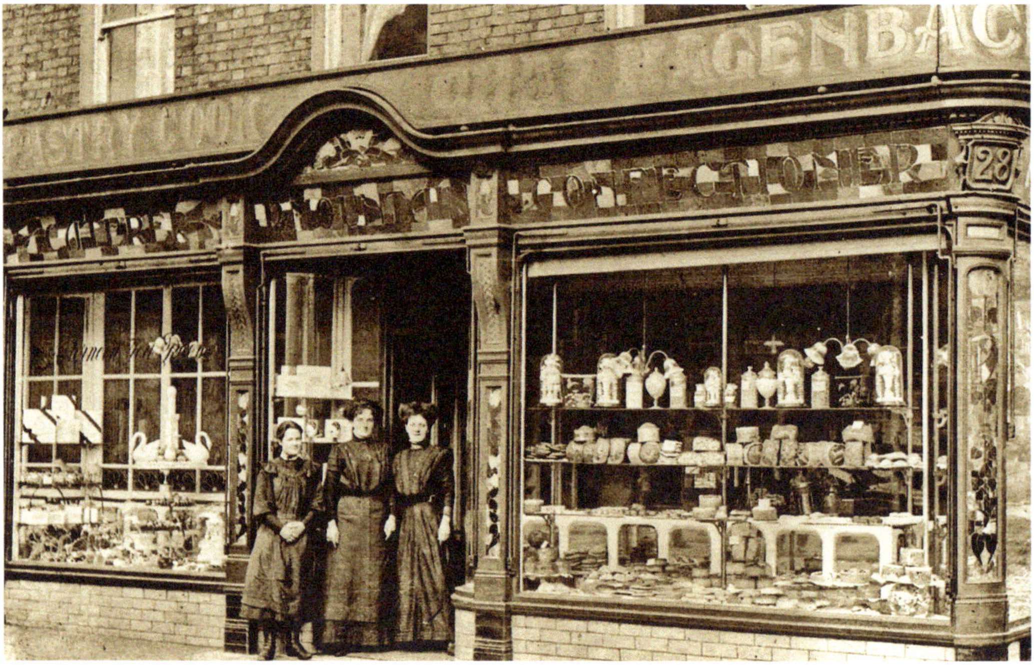

Above and below: Hagenbach's confectioners and bakers had a shop on the corner of Westmoreland Street and Union Street. The firm was founded by German immigrants at the end of the nineteenth century. The firm in the years after the Second World War built a large factory on Chald Lane and went into receivership in 1988.

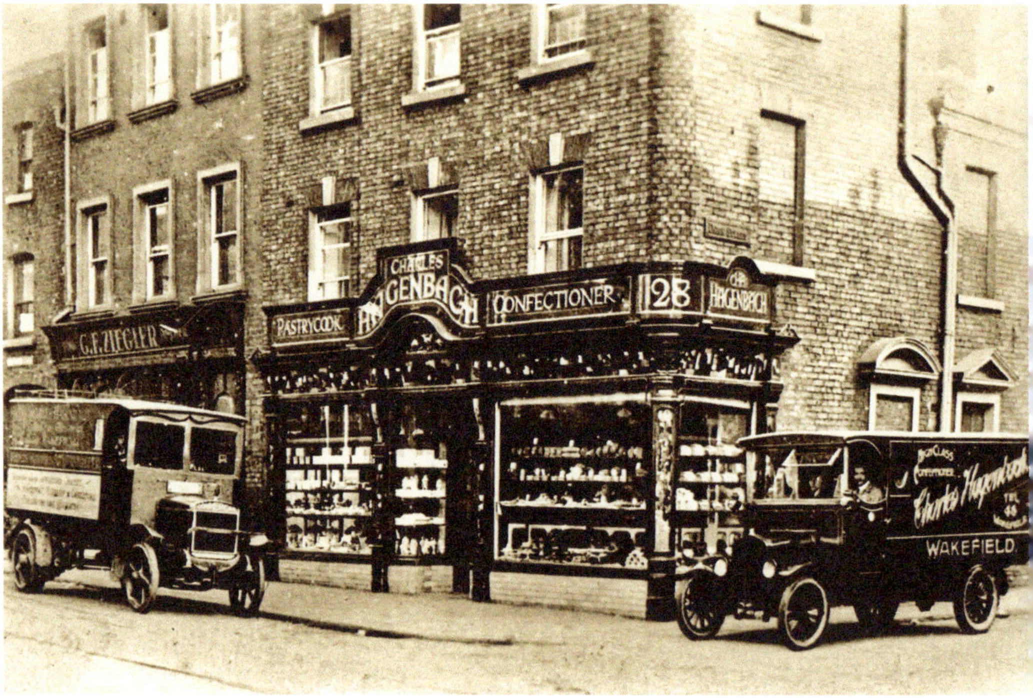

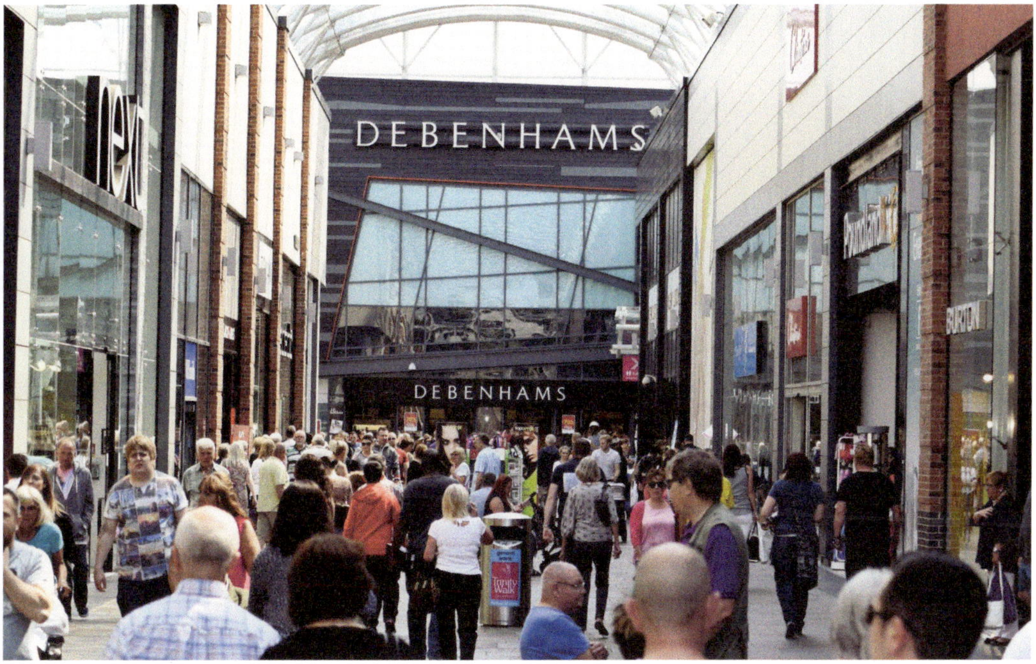

Above and below: The entrance to Trinity Walk Shopping Centre, the newest of several retail destinations in the city.

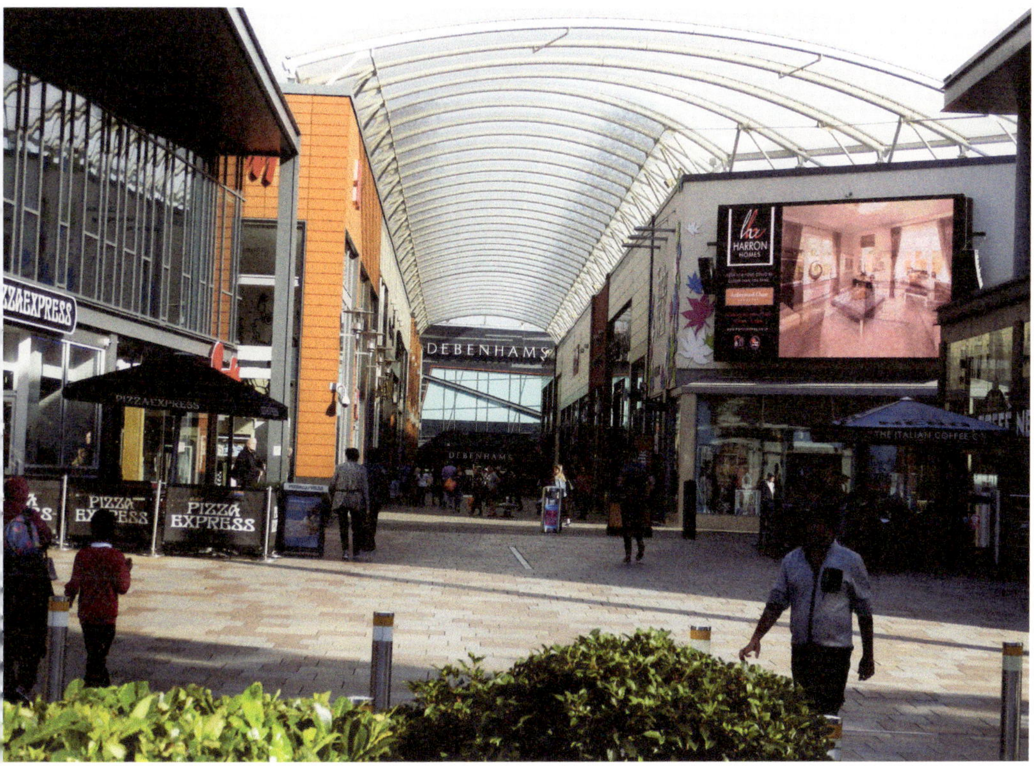

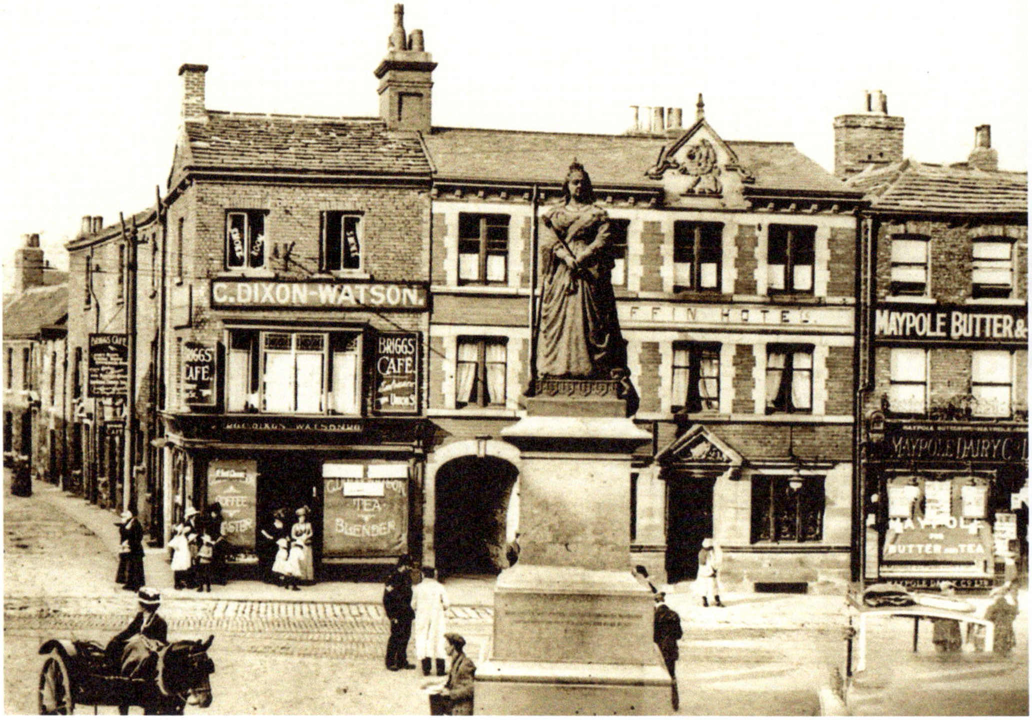

Shops on Westmoreland Street in the Bull Ring shortly after the unveiling of the statue of Queen Victoria.

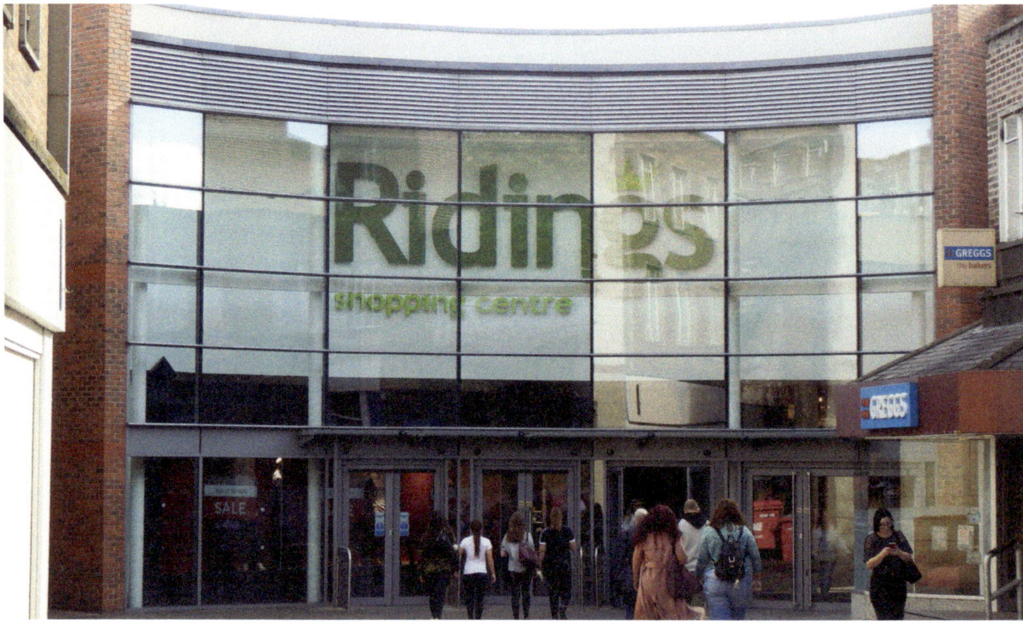

Entrance to the Ridings Shopping Centre – now over thirty years old.

BIBLIOGRAPHY

The bulk of this text is based on contemporary newspapers as well as extensive notes and MSS sources held by the late John Goodchild. The Crewe Muniment papers at Sheffield City Archives have been invaluable in helping unlock some of the Milnes family business. Also housed in Sheffield City Archives are the Wentworth Woodhouse papers, which includes thousands of letters to and from Marquis Rockingham, including many sent from and to the Milnes family and other members of Westgate Chapel. Further, the Yorkshire Association papers housed at York Library and Archives offers a direct insight into the life and politics of Jack Milnes. Published texts are as follows:

Clarkson, Henry, *Memories of Merry Wakefield* (Amethyst Press: Wakefield, 1985)

Dawson, Paul Lindsay, *Westgate Chapel Wakefield* (ABGI: Wakefield, 2018)

Dawson, Paul Lindsay, *Yorkshire Unitarianism and International Politics: 1770 to 1830* (ABGI: Wakefield, 2019)

Maw, Peter, 'Yorkshire and Lancashire Ascendant: England's Textile Exports to New York and Philadelphia, 1750–1805' in *The Economic History Review*, 63, 3 (2010), pp. 734–768

Smail, John, *Woollen Manufacturing in Yorkshire* (Boydell Press: 2001)

Wilson, Richard George, *Gentlemen Merchants: The Merchant Community in Leeds 1700–1830* (Manchester University Press: Manchester, 1971)

Wilson, R. G., 'The Denison's and Milneses: Eighteenth-Century Merchant Landowners' in J. T. Ward and R. G. Wilson (eds), *Land and Industry: The Landed Estate and the Industrial Revolution* (David and Charles: Newton Abbott, 1971)